天安门广场

天安门城楼一角

人民英雄纪念碑

华表

北海公园

北海濠濮间园林

北海白塔

北海静心园石桥

北海九龙壁

北海团城白皮松

景山万春亭

王府井商业街

人民大会堂

Contents
目　录

Tian'anmen 天安门　1

Lifestyle of the Modern City 现代都市风情 109

※ ※ ※

Tian'anmen

天安门

Tian'anmen is situated on the north-south axle in central Beijing. With Chang'an Boulevard running across its front, Tian'anmen Gate is not only connected with, but also stays aloof from other architecture on the square. As the main gate of the imperial palace of the Ming and Qing Dynasties, and symbol of Beijing and China today, Tian'anmen has experienced the vicissitudes of history. On visiting Beijing, every tourist, from either home or abroad, cannot help being greatly impressed by the magnificence of Tian'anmen gate and the imposing atmosphere of the entire square.

As Beijing's famous scenic spot, Tian'anmen gate, Tian'anmen Square and all other architecture there are vicwed as messengers of

Chinese culture by a growing number of Chinese and foreign tourists. For a better understanding of the past and present of Tian'anmen, let us begin our tour from Tian'anmen Square.

Key Words & Expressions

1. axle 轴线
2. boulevard 大道
3. aloof 远离
4. main gate 正门
5. symbol 象征
6. vicissitudes 变迁兴衰
7. magnificence 宏伟
8. imposing 壮观的
9. messengers 使者

Tian'anmen Square
天安门广场

The Largest of Its Kind in the World
世界名城中最大的广场

Like the Red Square in Moscow, the Arc De Triomphe in Paris and the Washington Monument, Tian'anmen Square is the symbolic architecture of Beijing. It was named "the largest public square in the world" evaluated at the "World Top Tourism in Beijing" in 1992. Millions of tourists are attracted to the square by its long history and splendid appearance, and it has become the very image of Beijing's charm to its many visitors.

Located on the central axle of Beijing, Tian' anmen Square begins from the northern red wall, reaches Zhengyangmen Gate Tower, or Front Gate, in the south and the Great Hall of the People in the west, and includes the Museum of Chinese History and the Museum of Chinese Revolution in the east. It is 880 meters from north to south, and 500 meters from east to west, and has a total area of 440, 000 square meters. As many as one million people can gather here at one time. It has witnessed the magnificent sight of the founding ceremony of the PRC and National Day military parades, and is the witness of every great leap forward by the country.

Key Words & Expressions

1. Red Square 红场
2. Arc De Triomphe 凯旋门
3. Washington Monument 华盛顿纪念碑
4. splendid 雄伟的

5. charm 魅力
6. Great Hall of the People 人民大会堂
7. Museum of Chinese History
   中国历史博物馆
8. Museum of Chinese Revolution
   中国革命博物馆
9. witness 见证
10. founding ceremony 开国大典
11. National Day 国庆节
12. military parades 阅兵
13. leap 飞跃

History of Tian'anmen Square

天安门广场的历史演变

Early in the Liao and Jin periods, Beijing became the political center of northern China, featuring the well-known Xingguo Temple, which was built near the present Zhongshan Park. When the Mongolian cavalry ruled the Central Plains, Beijing was built as the Yuan capital Dadu. Lizhengmen Gate, the due south gate of the external part of the city, was situated where the south of Tian' anmen Gate now is. In other words, Tian' anmen Square was the only way in and out of the capital as early as in the Yuan Dynasty. It was only after Yongle reign of the Ming Dynasty moved the capital to Beijing that the present - day Tian'anmen Square began to take shape.

In the 15th year of Yongle reign of the Ming Dynasty, Chengtianmen Gate, the main gate of the capital and today's Tian' anmen Gate, was completed. So was Damingmen Gate (renamed as Daqingmen Gate and Zhonghuamen Gate in Qing Dynasty and the Republic of China respectively), or the southernmost gate where the Memorial Hall of Chairman Mao is. The two red walls reached out from Damingmen Gate to the east and west respectively, then marched north, finally connected with Chengtianmen Gate, forming a T-shape square where royal activities took place in front of the Tian' anmen Gate Tower. This is the original Tian'anmen Square.

Early in the Republic of China, removing the ban of free crossing near the imperial city, the government constructed the east and west avenues of Tian' anmen Square and allowed citizens to pass between Shenwu Gate (Gate of Military Prowess) and Jingshan Mountain. Thus, the two main roads from north to south and east to west were linked. Later, with the demolition of some walls and side gates, a small square eventually came into being.

After the founding of the People's Republic of China, several enlargements were made to Tian'anmen Square.

Key Words & Expressions

1. Mongolian cavalry 蒙古骑兵
2. Due south gate 正南门
3. in other words 也就是说
4. take shape 成形
5. reign 统治时期
6. respectively 分别地
7. Tian'anmen Gate Tower 城楼
8. Gate of Military Prowess 神武门
9. Jingshan Mountain 景山
10. demolition 毁坏
11. eventually 最终
12. enlargement 扩建

Chessboard Street and Thousand-Step Corridor 天安门广场上的棋盘街与千步廊

The area from the south gate in the southern most part of Tian'anmen Square between the Memorial Hall of Chairman Mao and Zhengyangmen Gate Tower was referred to as Chessboard Street in Ming and Qing Dynasties. Enclosed by a wooden fence in the Ming Dynasty, the passage stretching from east to west in the middle looked like the borderline on a Chinese chessboard. During Qianlong reign of Qing Dynasty, renovations were made to the street, with a square stone fence replacing the original wooden one. Then, the street was shaped more like a *weiqi* chessboard. Once the commercial and recreation center of the Ming and Qing Dynasties, Chessboard Street was also called Tianjie Street(Imperial Street) as ordinary citizens felt it was a great pleasure to sell snacks, perform acrobatics and opera near the Forbidden City.

Thousand – Step Corridor runs along the east, west and south of the T – shape square in Daqingmen Gate, (the current Memorial Hall of Chairman Mao), with white marble stairs and 144 courtrooms. The Left Chang'an Gate and East Thousand – Step Corridor witnessed the successes of those few chosen by the emperor in the imperial examinations. In the past, successful candidates would be summoned two days after the final imperial examination, which was presided over by the emperor himself. Then, the list of successful candidates would be put up in a temporary Dragon Shed by the candidates and officials of the Ministry of Rites out of the Left Chang'an

Gate. Seeing their names on the list, the candidates were mostly wreathed in smiles. In the Chinese saying "carp leaping into the dragon's gate", people referred to the Left Chang'an Gate as the Dragon Gate. The Right Chang'an Gate and West Thousand-Step Corridor were where autumn and court trials were held. The charged usually went into the square through the Right Chang'an Gate to be up for trial. Those sentenced to death would then be sent to Caishikou out of Xuanwumen Gate to be executed on the morning of the Winter Solstice. In most cases, prisoners passing through the Right Chang'an Gate had little chance of living. Therefore, the gate was given the name Tiger Gate (jaws of death). With the successes of candidates in the imperial examinations and executions of prisoners both taking place here, it is evident that the destiny of ordinary citizens was in the hands of the emperor.

Key Words & Expressions

1. Chessboard Street 棋盘街
2. Thousand-step corridor 千步廊
3. Memorial Hall of Chairman Mao 毛主席纪念堂
4. enclosed 围着的

5. borderline 边界线
6. renovation 修葺
7. *weiqi* chessboard 围棋棋盘
8. snack 小吃
9. acrobatics 杂技
10. marble 大理石
11. imperial examinations 科举考试
12. temporary 暂时的
13. Dragon Shed 龙棚
14. Winter Solstice 冬至
15. Tiger Gate 虎门
16. destiny 命运

White Lilacs and Yellow Roses
昔日广场上的白丁香与黄刺玫

When rambling on the vast square, how can we guess that white lilacs and yellow roses flourished here several decades ago, instead of today's artificial lawns and ornamental flowers?

After the Revolution of 1911, China sank into entangled warfare. Japanese invaders ravished Beijing for eight years, leaving ruins everywhere. At that critical moment, Tian'anmen Square was the important stage for the people's patriotic movement. The feudal warlords and Kuomintang rulers planted many white lilacs and yellow roses in front of the square, to reduce its size and prohibit demonstrations. These beautiful flowers hence became synonyms for conspiracy and evil.

Key Words & Expressions

1. lilac 丁香
2. ramble 漫步
3. flourish 茂盛
4. Revolution of 1911 辛亥革命
5. entangled warfare 混战
6. ravish 掠夺
7. patriotic 爱国的
8. feudal warlords 封建军阀
9. Kuomintang 国民党
10. conspiracy 阴谋

Extensions and Opening of Tian'anmen Square 天安门广场的扩建与开放

Three major extensions have been carried out since the founding of the People's Republic of China. The first renovation of the original square took place in 1949, right after the founding of the PRC. Later, for the celebration of the 10th anniversary, the largest-scale extension took place in 1958 and the current 880-meter-long and 500-meter-wide square finally took shape. The Great

Hall of the People, Monument to the People's Heroes, Museum of Chinese History and Museum of Chinese Revolution were all built then. Then, after the great Chairman Mao passed away in 1976, a Memorial Hall was erected between the Monument to the People's Heroes and Zhengyangmen Gate to express the deep sorrow of the people of China. After the three extensions, today's Tian'anmen Square in central Beijing demonstrates the uniqueness of Chinese culture.

Key Words & Expressions

1. extension 扩建
2. anniversary 周年纪念
3. current 现在的
4. Monument to the People's Heroes
   人民英雄纪念碑
5. erect 建立
6. uniqueness 独特

Flag-Raising and Flag-Lowering Ceremonies 天安门广场上的升降旗仪式

Since May 1, 1991, regulations issued by the Beijing municipality began to be enforced. They stipulate that on the first, 11th and 21st day of each month and on important national festivals (such as New Year's Day, Spring

Festival, International Labor Day, the founding day of the Party, Army Day and National Day), flag – raising and flag – lowering ceremonies are to be held and the national anthem be played by the military band. On other days, ceremonies shall also take place and a recording of the national anthem is to be played. Since then, the flag – raising and flag – lowering ceremony has become a favorite event for both domestic and foreign tourists.

The 32.6 – meter – tall flagpole, made from a seamless steel pipe by the Shougang Group, weighs seven tons. Undergoing special processing, it can remain rustproof for 20 years.

Every day, accompanied by the majestic and resonant sound of the national anthem, the bright – colored five – star flag rises slowly with the sunrise, symbolizing the bright future for China. The flag – lowering ceremony is held at sunset. It takes two minutes and seven seconds to raise the flag to the top of the pole. The ceremony has become an important sight for tourists visiting Tian'anmen Square. For the convenience of tourists, an announcement of the time for the ceremony of the following day is made daily. Led by the flag being carried by one soldier and guarded by two others, the team of 96 (symbolizing protecting China's 9.6-million-sq. km territory) soldiers in uniform, shouldering semi-automatic rifles, march firmly out of Tian'anmen Gate to majestic martial music. Their orderly 138-step march from the Golden water Bridge to the flagpole clearly bespeaks the strong mind of the Chinese people and the illustrious image of the nation.

Key Words & Expressions

1. Flag-raising and flag-lowering ceremonies 升降旗仪式
2. regulation 规章
3. municipality 市政当局
4. Spring Festival 春节
5. International Labor Day 国际劳动节
6. Army Day 建军节
7. national anthem 国歌
8. seamless 无缝的
9. rustproof 不会生锈的
10. accompany 伴奏
11. resonant 嘹亮的
12. semi-automatic 半自动的
13. majestic 雄壮的
14. Golden Water Bridge 金水桥

15. flagpole 旗杆
16. bespeak 显示
17. illustrious image 光辉形象

Tian'anmen Gate Tower 天安门城楼

Architectural Characteristics and Major Functions 天安门城楼的建筑特色及主要作用

We usually refer to Tian' anmen Gate Tower as Tian' anmen. Construction first commenced in 1417, in the 15th year of Yongle reign of the Ming Dynasty, and it was completed three years later. Tian'anmen Gate Tower was the main entrance to the imperial city of the Ming and Qing Dynasties. Originally named Chengtianmen Gate, meaning by the Grace of God, Tian' anmen Gate was regarded as an important place for the emperor to worship God. Originally a wooden arch with six pillars and five doors, it was reconstructed into a nine - room wide and five - room-deep gate tower after a ruinous fire (the number nine and five embodies the supremacy of the emperor). However, it was destroyed again by warfare at the end of the Ming Dynasty. It was renamed as Tian' anmen Gate after its reconstruction in 1651, the eighth year of emperor Shunzhi' s reign of the Qing Dynasty. Emperor Shunzhi renamed the three front halls of the Forbidden City the Hall of Supreme Harmony, the Hall of Middle Harmony and the Hall of Preserving Harmony, all containing the character he (harmony); and the four gates of the imperial city Tian'anmen Gate, Di'anmen Gate, Dong'anmen Gate and Xi'anmen Gate, all with the word an (peace), expressing his best wishes for the nation to be harmonious and peaceful.

The 34.7 - meter - high Tian' anmen Gate is composed of a base, arch and tower. The base is 1.59 meters high and the arch, made from stone blocks, with each weighing 420 kg, is 14.6 meters in height. There are six small yellow - tiled rooms with red walls and windows at the eastern and western sides of the gate tower, for soldiers guarding Tian' anmen Gate.

In the Ming and Qing Dynasties, on occasions of important ceremonies, such as the sacrifices to Heaven on Winter Solstice and to Earth on Summer Solstice, praying for grain in spring, the emperor's wedding and dispatch of soldiers; the emperor and his attendants usually went through Tian'anmen Gate. Ceremonies of issuing the imperial edict were held on the Tian'anmen Gate Tower when the emperor claimed the throne, married the empress and crowned the prince.

After the founding of the PRC, leaders of the nation would march to Tian'anmen Gate Tower to celebrate with the people for such grand ceremonies as the founding ceremony and celebration of National Day.

Key Words & Expressions

1. refer to 提到
2. commence 开始
3. worship 崇拜
4. ruinous 破坏性的
5. Hall of Supreme Harmony 太和殿
6. Hall of Middle Harmony 中和殿
7. Hall of Preserving Harmony 保和殿
8. yellow-tiled 黄瓦的
9. sacrifices to Heaven 祭天
10. dispatch 派遣
11. attendant 随员
12. imperial edict 诏书

Tian'anmen Gate Tower and Golden Phoenix Issuing Edict 天安门城楼与"金凤颁诏"

The ceremony for issuing the imperial edict in the Ming and Qing Dynasties were referred to as Golden Phoenix Issuing Edict. In the Ming Dynasty, a dragon-headed pole tied with colorful cord would be put down along the wall. In the Qing Dynasty, an altar for issuing the edict was erected in the middle of the Tian'anmen Gate Tower. Having read it out to other officials performing a kowtow, the official usually put the edict onto a gilded cloud-shaped plate and tied it, with a yellow silk thread, into the mouth of a wooden carved golden phoenix. The phoenix then "flew" slowly down from the tower, symbolizing the imperial edict landed from Heaven onto earth. Officials from the Ministry of Rites accepted the edict with the plate and put it into the dragon pavilion before sending to the Ministry of Rites, which was responsible for the printing and publication of the edict. The whole process was called Golden Phoenix Issuing Edict.

On February 12, 1912, a ceremony was held to issue the abdication edict of the last emperor Puyi. The Revolution of 1911 toppled the Qing Dynasty, but the issuing of the abdication of the last emperor did not take place until 1912. Written on ordinary paper in ink, the 53-cm-long and 21.5-cm-wide edict still followed the procedure of the Golden Phoenix Issuing Edict. However, the royal family could no longer be as extravagant as before, as they could only continue residing in the previous imperial palace because of the special treatment of the new government. The last Golden Phoenix Issuing Edict withdrew from the stage of history in such a gloomy way.

Key Words & Expressions

1. Golden Phoenix Issuing Edict
   金凤颁诏
2. kowtow 叩头
3. gilded 镀金的
4. Ministry of Rites 礼部
5. abdication 退位
6. topple 推翻
7. withdraw from 退出

Red Lanterns Hung High
“大红灯笼高高挂”

Walking on Tian'anmen Square, we can see the new palace lantern hung on the gate tower. Many people may have seen the original eight red lanterns that once hung there from a documentary about the founding ceremony of the PRC, or in other pictures. They were put into use for the founding ceremony, and witnessing the growth of China. You may wonder where they are now.

Just prior to National Day 1994, the current lanterns replaced them. Three of the original eight were kept by the administrative committee of Tian' anmen and relevant museum. The two in the east and west were auctioned for 13.8 million yuan, which was donated to Project Hope and the water project of the poor mountainous areas of Beijing. The largest palace lanterns in history, each was 2.23 meters in height, 8.05 meters in circumference, 2.25 meters in diameter and weighed 80 kg. To our surprise, the designers turned out to be Japanese, showing that the people of the two nations have had continuous friendly cultural exchanges.

Key Words & Expressions

1. palace lantern 宫灯
2. documentary 记录片
3. administrative committee 管理委员会
4. Project Hope 希望工程

Portrait of Chairman Mao

城楼上的毛主席肖像

On the central gate of Tian'anmen hangs a portrait of beloved Chairman Mao. Two huge posters overlooked the square; the one in the west reads Long Live the PRC. The other in the east reads Long Live the Union of World People. The framed portrait, six meters high, 4.6 meters wide and 1.5 tons in weight, is on record as being the nation's biggest hand - drawn portrait. For fear of weathering, it is usually replaced by a new one before each National Day.

Key Words & Expressions

1. portrait 肖像
2. poster 标语
3. Long Live the Union of World People 世界人民大团结万岁
4. weathering 风吹雨淋

Tian'anmen Gate Tower and Founding Ceremony of PRC 天安门城楼与开国大典

The founding of the People's Republic of China is of great significance in China's history, which turned over a new leaf with the solemn announcement of Chairman Mao --- The People's Republic of China is founded!

When Chairman Mao raised the five-star red flag on Tian' anmen Square, 300, 000 people stood in salute, shining with happiness. This scene must remain fresh in their memory even today.

Key Words & Expressions

1. turn over a new leaf 翻开新的一页
2. solemn 庄严的
3. five-star red flag 五星红旗
4. salute 致敬

Three Shells in Tian'anmen Gate Tower
天安门城楼上的三发炮弹

As the symbolic architecture of central Beijing, the Tian'anmen Gate Tower recorded both the happiness of founding day and humiliation in the past.

Workers found three bullet shells in a wooden beam in the west of the gate tower during reconstruction in 1952. The dimly visible English characters on them reminded us of the cruelty of the attack by the Eight-Power Allied Force.

Under feudalistic and imperialistic oppression, Chinese people launched the Yihetuan Movement (Boxer Uprising) in 1900. Owing to the cowardice and inability of the Qing

Dynasty, the Eight - Power Allied Force, comprised of over 2, 000 English, French, German, American, Japanese, Italian, Austrian and Russian soldiers, trampled into Beijing. Having burnt down the embrasure watchtower of Zhengyangmen Gate, they concentrated shooting at Tian' anmen, even destroyed the mouth of a carved *chi* (ancient legendary animal) on the roof of the Royal Ancestral Temple nearby. The three shells discovered is proof of their crime.

Key Words & Expressions

1. humiliation 耻辱
2. shell 炮弹
3. dimly visible 隐约可见的
4. Eight - Power Allied Force 八国联军
5. imperialistic 帝国主义的
6. Boxer Uprising 义和团运动
7. embrasure watchtower 箭楼
8. Royal Ancestral Temple 太庙

Opening of Tian'anmen Gate Tower

天安门城楼的开放

Once the main entrance to the imperial city of the Ming and Qing Dynasties, the Tian' men Gate Tower runs directly to the Forbidden City, out of the reach of ordinary citizens. Marching on the gate tower was totally out of the question for ordinary citizens. Even after the founding of the PRC, they still were denied access to the gate tower, though allowed to visit the Forbidden City. It was not until New Year' s Day 1988 that the gate tower was first opened to people from all over the world. The first Chinese visitor to ascend it was a 75-year-old Beijinger, and the first foreign tourists were a French couple, both received a cloisonné vase and a certificate in memory of this unusual day.

Key Words & Expressions

1. out of the question 不可能
2. access 接近
3. cloisonné vase 景泰蓝花瓶

Outer Golden Water River and Outer Golden Water Bridge 外金水河与外金水桥

Origin of the Name of the Golden Water River and Its Main Function 金水河名称的由来及主要作用

According to the theory of *Yin* and

Yang, gold should be situated in the west. As the river zigzagged from west to east in front of Tian'anmen, it was referred to as the Golden Water River. Since there is also a golden water river in the Forbidden City, this one was accordingly called the Outer Golden Water River, and the one in the Forbidden City the Inner Golden Water River. Not only adding fresh elements to its boring architectural style, mostly red walls and yellow tiles, the river also provides water for extinguishing fires in the palace and released water during summer downpours.

Key Words & Expressions

1. Outer Golden Water River 外金水河
2. theory of *Yin* and *Yang* 阴阳五行之说
3. Inner Golden Water River 内金水河
4. boring 枯燥的
5. extinguishing fire 灭火
6. downpour 暴雨

Lotuses and Coiling Dragons Indicating the Grade 荷花、蟠龙见等级

Seven white, lovely stone bridges cross the rippling blue Outer Golden Water River. The middle five, including the central Outer Golden River Bridge, are directly opposite the five gateways of Tian' anmen. With tall and narrow arches, the bridges display the beauty of arcs. Observant visitors may discover that the carved designs on the white marble railings of the bridge in the middle are coiled dragons, whereas those of the others are vivid lotuses. The variation reveals the different functions and grades of the bridges.

The one in the very middle, the imperial bridge, served for the passage of the emperors in the Ming and Qing Dynasties. Accordingly, the decoration of coiled dragon symbolizes the supremacy of the imperial power. The other four, with lotus ornamentation, vary in function. The two closest to the imperial bridge, or the noble' s bridges, were for the exclusive use of the royal family, while the other two were for the passage of high civil and military officials above grade - three. In addition, the two outmost bridges in front of Zhongshan Park and the Working People' s Cultural Palace served for the passage of officials under grade - four, soldiers, workers, maids and eunuchs. The rule of the grades must be strictly observed.

Upon the occasion of sacrificial ceremonies of the emperor in the Qing Dynasty, attendants and honor guards should go out through Tian' anmen Gate in five rows, and then pass the stone bridges in seven rows accordingly. However, this rule was only for the occasion when the emperor was present. When going to or withdrawing from the court, all officials took the outermost bridges.

Key Words & Expressions

1. rippling 起涟漪的
2. gateway 门洞
3. arc 弧线
4. railing 栏杆
5. coiled dragon 蟠龙
6. lotus 莲花
7. supremacy 至高
8. eunuch 太监
9. outermost 最外面的

The Stone Lion
石狮

The Lion and the Dragon 狮子与龙子

A pair of white marble lions stand at the end of the Golden Water Bridge. Atrocious and strong lions were said to be the king of animals in ancient China. Later, folklore even called the lion as the eighth son of the dragon, or Suanni in Chinese. Since Suanni favored fire, it was used as a decoration on incense burners. Gradually, the lion became the representative of supreme imperial power. Standing in front of the gate of the imperial palace, it usually served to ward off evil as a symbol of stateliness and holiness.

Male and Female Lions 雄狮与雌狮

Sitting majestically in front of Tian' anmen, the male stone lion on the left steps onto a big silk ball, embodying the vast land and supreme power of the emperor. The female lion on the right, with a cute little lion cub at her left foot, symbolizes the graceful empress. Ignoring the tiny difference at their feet, visitors may find it hard to tell them apart. It was said that lions in ancient China were mainly tributes from foreign countries, so no wonder stonemasons differentiated them with a silk ball and the little lion cub. Situated in front of the Golden River, the pair of stone lions witnessed every slight change that has been happening here. They may be proud of the great changes of Beijing.

Key Words & Expressions

1. cloud pillar 华表
2. atrocious 凶猛的
3. folklore 民间传说

4. ward off evil 驱邪
5. majestically 威严地
6. embody 代表
7. tell …apart 区分开
8. cute 可爱的
9. stonemason 石匠

Huabiao and Suggestion Wooden Stake
华表与“诽谤木”

There is a pair of ornamental 10 - meter - high stone pillars meticulously carved from marble standing in front and behind Tian' anmen, or our familiar Huabiao (cloud pillar) in Chinese. It has a long history in China. As the legend goes, it served as road mark early in the Yao and Shun Age in primitive society. According to historical records, emperor Shun allowed ordinary citizens to carve suggestions on a wooden stake, wishing to learn the situation of the people and reduce mistakes. Consequently, the wooden stake was referred to as the Suggestion Wood. As time went on, this way of learning public opinions gradually became out - of - date. Thus, the original wooden stake changed into the present white marble carving, with the pattern of dragon and clouds as a symbol of imperial power, put in front of imperial palaces or tombs.

Key Words & Expressions

1. ornamental 装饰性的
2. road mark 路标
3. wooden stake 木桩
4. Suggestion Wood 诽谤木

Legendary Animal on Huabiao (Cloud Pillar)
华表上的"望天犼"

There is a monstrous legendary animal standing on the round plate of Huabiao, and a coiled dragon with four feet and five claws flies on the rolling clouds in the middle of the stone pillar. Around the octagonal Buddhist novice base is a square stone fence, with a little stone lion sitting on each side. The entire Huabiao, including the base, is 9.57 meters in height. It was said that the legendary animal standing high on the Huabiao kept an eye on all actions taken by the emperor. It would warn him to return to court affairs if he paid private visit out of the palace for too long. The two facing south were there to warn the emperor to return, whereas the two facing north, the direction of the Forbidden City, gazed at the imperial harem. If the emperor abandoned himself to the comforts of the imperial harem, they would expostulate with him about the situation of the people.

Key Words & Expressions

1. monstrous 凶猛的
2. octagonal 八角形的
3. kept an eye on 密切注视
4. imperial harem 后宫
5. expostulate 劝诫

Transfer of Huabiao

华表"搬家"

The Huabiao is now situated six meters behind the original site. You may wonder why and how it was moved.

To answer this question, we have to first clarify the history of the invasion of the Eight-Power Allied Force, which bombarded the Tiananmen Gate Tower, the embrasure watchtower and the gate tower of Qianmen Gate with fierce shellfire on at the night of August 13, 1900. As a result, the wall collapsed and the Huabiao at the west side fell. After the founding of the PRC and due to the extension project of Tiananmen Square, the over 20, 000-kg renovated Huabiao must be moved back six meters, without incurring damages.

A 64 - year - old man, Xu Rong, finally accomplished this challenging task. Having ancestors responsible for building the framework for the palace, Xu Rong himself was engaged in making the gold casket for the emperor. Adopting the same method used to transfer the gold casket, he moved the Huabiao to its present place with wooden stakes, cords and hoisting chains. The unique talent of the working people is the source of every piece of outstanding work.

Key Words & Expressions

1. clarify 阐明
2. bombard 炮轰
3. collapse 倒塌
4. incur 招致
5. casket 棺材
6. hoisting chain 吊链

Monument to the People's Heroes
人民英雄纪念碑

Monument and the Inscriptions
碑体及碑文介绍

Located to the south of the five - star red

flag of Tian' anmen Square, the monument was erected in memory of the people's heroes who sacrificed their lives for the revolution between 1840 and 1949. Designed by Liang Sicheng, construction began August 1, 1952, and it was completed in April 1958. Made from 17,000 pieces of granites and white marble, it is 37.94 meters in height and covers an area of 3, 000 sq meters. Constructed from a complete piece of granite, the main part of the monument is 14.7 meters long, 2.9 meters wide, one meter thick and weighs 103 tons. Standing upright and stately at the center of the square, it is situated 440 meters away from the wall base of the square.

Directly facing Tian' anmen Gate, eight gilded characters written by the late Chairman Mao are inscribed at the center of the tablet, stating Immortality to the People' s Heroes. On the obverse side of the tablet is an inscription by the late Prime Minster Zhou Enlai. It says, Immortality to the Martyrs in the Liberation War and Revolution during the Past Three Years! Immortality to the Martyrs in the Liberation War and Revolution during the Past Thirty Years! Immortality to the Martyrs against the Enemy and for National Independence and the People's Freedom and Happiness after 1840!

Key Words & Expressions

1. granite 花岗岩
2. inscribe 记下
3. tablet 碑
4. Immortality to the People's Heroes 人民英雄永垂不朽
5. Martyr 烈士
6. Liberation War 解放战争

Top of the Tablet and Design
碑顶和浮雕图案

With layers of curtains on rolling clouds, the top of the monument embodies the traditional architectural style and major pattern of the tablet. The design was finally determined, outlined by famous historian Fan Wenlan, examined by Chairman Mao and discussed many times by the Party Central Committee. In historic order, eight events were to be depicted: the Opium War, Jintian Uprising, Wuchang Uprising, the May Fourth Movement, the May 30th Movement, Nanchang Uprising, War of Resistance Against Japanese Aggression and the Successful Crossing the Yangtze River. Completed by eight experts and their assistants, the design is two meters high and 40.68 meters long.

Ornamental figures comprising red stars, pines and cypresses and flags were carved at the top of the eastern and western sides of the tablet, symbolizing the lasting revolutionary spirit. Eight wreaths of peonies, lotuses and chrysanthemums around the base were carved as symbol of nobleness, pureness and perseverance to show respect to the heroes.

Key Words & Expressions

1. Party Central Committee 党中央
2. Opium War 鸦片战争
3. Jintian Uprising 金田起义
4. Wuchang Uprising 武昌起义
5. May Fourth Movement 五四运动
6. War of Resistance Against Japanese Aggression 抗日游击战争
7. Successful Crossing the Yangtze River 胜利渡江
8. Cypress 柏树
9. Chrysanthemum 菊花

Gilded Characters of Immortality to the People's Heroes "人民英雄永垂不朽"镏金文字

The eight gilded characters on the obverse side of the monument were written by the late

Chairman Mao and magnified 20 times. The character "*Yong*" is over two meters high. Adopting a traditional gold - plating technique, the characters will not fade. The eight characters and inscriptions consumed 6.5 kg of gold, revealing the excellence of the gold - plating technique.

Key Words & Expressions

1. obverse 正面
2. magnify 放大
3. gold - plating technique 镏金工艺

Memorial Hall of Chairman Mao 毛主席纪念堂

Introduction 简介

The great leader Chairman Mao passed away on Sept. 9, 1976. The central government determined to build a memorial hall to preserve Chairman Mao's body. Located between the Monument to the People's Heroes and Zhengyangmen Gate, the memorial hall faces north, opposite Tian'anmen Gate. The foundation was laid on Nov. 24, 1976 and the hall completed the following May. Covering an area of 28, 000 sq meters, the hall is supported by 44 octagonal granite pillars. Two groups of 8.7 - meter - high carvings have been erected in the courtyard. The grand architecture embodies the greatness of Chairman Mao.

Key Words & Expressions

1. passed away 逝世
2. was determined to 决定
3. opposite 在……对面
4. courtyard 庭院

Central Viewing Hall 中央瞻仰厅

In the central hall, the northern part of the memorial hall, is a seated white marble statue, 3.45 meters in height. Constructed with more than 40 sq - meter stones, the statue took workers more than six months to complete. The kindly countenance and tall stature add to the chairman's amiability.

Right behind the statue hangs a huge wool tapestry, depicting the beautiful scenery of China, indicating the great foresight of Chairman Mao. It took 43 embroiderers 58 days and nights to finish it. Nearly 300 - kg of wool and 6.4 million stitches went into the 7 - meter - high, 24 - meter - long work.

Over 1, 200 different colors, coupled with the first use of gold thread and colorful wool thread bespeaks the advanced level of China's embroidery techniques.

A key part of the memorial hall, right in the very center of the viewing hall, is the crystal casket of Chairman Mao on a black granite stone pedestal, surrounded by flowers. Covered by the flag of the Communist Party, the body of Chairman Mao appeared composed and solemn. The crystal casket is waterproof, dustproof and shockproof. It rises for visitors to view, and later descends back underground, conducing to the preservation of the body. The silk flowers and pine branches around the body are waterproof, dustproof and long-lasting, representing the lasting image of Chairman Mao in people's minds.

Key Words & Expressions

1. foundation 地基
2. Central Viewing Hall 中央瞻仰厅
3. statue 雕像
4. stature 身高
5. countenance 面容
6. amiability 和蔼可亲
7. wool tapestry 绒绣壁毯
8. stitch 针脚

9. embroidery 刺绣
10. crystal casket 水晶棺
11. composed and solemn 安详而肃穆
12. waterproof 防水的
13. dustproof 防尘的
14. shockproof 防震的

Opening of the Memorial Hall of Chairman Mao and Exhibition Halls of Achievements of Other Leaders 纪念堂的开放及其他领袖人物的纪念室

The memorial hall opened to the public on Sept. 9, 1977, one year after Chairman Mao's death. At first, visitors had to buy an admission ticket, but this was cancelled on July 1, 1984. Since then, visitors lined up to view Chairman Mao's body at no charge. The first foreign leader to visit the memorial hall was Tito, Yugoslav Statesman. Tens of thousands of people have queued to view Chairman Mao's body with reverence, and the memorial hall has become the base of revolutionary education.

After the deaths of several leaders, exhibition halls featuring the revolutionary achievements of Chairman Mao, Liu Shaoqi, Zhou Enlai and Zhu De were constructed in

1988 on the eastern and western sides of the memorial hall, displaying many cultural relics, pictures, letters and documents. In recent years, the memorial halls of Deng Xiaoping and Chen Yun were also established.

Key Words & Expressions

1. admission ticket 门票
2. cancel 取消
3. Tito 铁托
4. queue 排队

Qianmen Gate (Zhengyangmen Gate) 前门(正阳门)

City Gates of Beijing 北京的城门

Beijing city in the Ming and Qing Dynasties consisted of four parts—the outer city, the inner city, the imperial city and the palace, each of which was enclosed by thick city walls. Tian'anmen Gate was once the main entrance to the imperial city, the Meridian Gate to the palace and the present Qianmen Gate or Zhengyangmen Gate to the inner city. The original city wall of the inner city was geographically equivalent to today's second-ring road. The names of the nine stations along the metro line were the nine gates of the inner city, Qianmen Gate, Chongwenmen Gate, Xuanwumen Gate, Fuchengmen Gate, Xizhimen Gate, Deshengmen Gate, Andingmen Gate, Dongzhimen Gate and Chaoyangmen Gate. After the founding of the PRC, almost all of the city's walls and gates were demolished to further city planning. Of the original inner city, only Zhengyangmen Gate and Deshengmen Gate were preserved.

There were strict rules to follow regarding the use of the inner city in the Ming and Qing Dynasty. Zhengyangmen Gate, the main entrance, served for the exclusive passage of carts of the royal family. Wine carts could pass through Chongwenmen Gate, prison vans via Xuanwumen Gate, coal carts through Fuchengmen Gate, water carts via Xizhimen Gate, chariots through Deshengmen Gate, dung-carts via Andingmen Gate, lumber carts through Dongzhimen Gate and grain carts via Chaoyangmen Gate. Different carts had to go through the correct gate in the right order.

Key Words & Expressions

1. city gate 城门
2. Meridian Gate 午门
3. geographically 地理上地
4. equivalent to 相当于
5. cart 车
6. via 通过

Zhengyangmen Gate and Its Function

正阳门及其作用

Among the nine gates of the inner city, Zhengyangmen Gate, the current Qianmen Gate, is the most famous. As in ancient China the south was situated in the yang direction or the positive (Zheng in Chinese) side, the gate in the south was referred to as Zhengyangmen Gate. Its location in front of the Forbidden City gave it another name — — — Qianmen Gate.

Built in 1420, the 18th year of Yongle reign of the Ming Dynasty, Zhengyangmen Gate is 42 meters in height. The main gate on the northern side, which is the gate tower of Zhengyangmen Gate and the embrasure watchtower with many arrow windows, was the highest.

As the highest - leveled, Zhengyangmen

Gate was also called the national gate. Usually closed, the middle of the three gates was opened only for the emperor's passage, although this was not the case for the death of the emperor. Hence, the gate was called the auspicious gate, and exclusively used on the emperor's wedding.

Stationed with soldiers, the embrasure watchtower has many apertures for arrows and artillery installed to defend against the enemy and guard the imperial city. However, it almost killed the last Emperor Zhu Youjian of Chongzhen reign of the Ming Dynasty. He once marched toward Zhengyangmen Gate with 400 bodyguards. Uninformed of the emperor's arrival, the stationed soldiers mistook them as rebels and fired at the emperor, who barely escaped death.

Every time a rebel army attacked Beijing, a warning lamp would be hung upon Qianmen Gate Tower to report the situation of the battle outside the city. One lamp indicated that the enemy was getting closer; two indicated that it was a fierce battle, and three showed that rebels were capturing the city. The last emperor did not leave to hang himself on Jinshan Mountain until three lamps were hung on the Qianmen Gate Tower.

Key Words & Expressions

1. national gate 国门
2. Aperture 孔
3. artillery 炮
4. Barely 仅仅

Series of Exhibitions of Old Beijing City

老北京系列展览

The embrasure watchtower and gate tower of Zhengyangmen Gate were opened to the public in 1990 and 1991 respectively. Standing on the ancient - styled Qianmen Gate Tower, you can experience both the bustling Dazhalan commercial street and the solemnity and holiness of Tiananmen Square. A series of exhibitions depicting the folk arts of old Beijing, including pictures, models and handicrafts describing the life of ordinary Beijing citizens, seem to bring tourists back to a life experienced decades, or even hundreds of years ago. Photographic and newspaper exhibitions are also held here.

Key Words & Expressions

1. bustling 熙熙攘攘的
2. Photographic exhibitions 摄影展

Zhongshan Park
中山公园

History 演变

Originally the sacrificial altar in the Ming and Qing Dynasties, Zhongshan Park is located to the west of Tian' anmen. Reconstructed on the old site of the Yuan Dynasty Wanshouxingguo Temple, it served for sacrificial rites to the God of Earth and the God of Grain. It became a central park in 1914 and renamed as Zhongshan Park in honor of Sun Yat - sen in 1928. Facing Tian' anmen Square, Zhongshan Park and Working People's Cultural Palace are symmetrical. It is not only an old park, but also a place to host important political and cultural activities.

Key Words & Expressions

1. sacrificial altar 祭坛
2. rite 仪式
3. God of Earth 土地神
4. God of Grain 五谷神
5. Sun Yat - sen 孙中山
6. Working People's Cultural Palace 劳动人民文化宫

Kettler Memorial Archway
克林德碑

A white marble memorial archway greets visitors walking into through the southern gate of Zhongshan Park. Decorated with four characters that say Defending Peace, it has witnessed our people's struggle against imperialistic oppression for the past hundred years.

With the invasion of the Eight - Power Allied Force into Beijing in 1900, the German minister Kettler affronted the Yihetuan and was beaten to death. The corrupt and incapable Qing Dynasty not only offered an apology to Germany, but also built an archway in Dongzongbu lane in Dongdan. After WWI in 1918, the victorious countries renamed the archway the Archway of the Success of Truth, due to the defeat of Germany, and moved it into Zhongshan Park. The Asian - Pacific peace meeting in 1952 finally renamed it the Archway Defending Peace, the name it still retains.

Key Words & Expressions

1. Kettler Memorial Archway 克林德碑
2. affront 冒犯

3. Corrupt 腐败的
4. Archway of the Success of Truth 公理战胜坊

Xili (Learning Rites) Pavilion
习礼亭

Built in 1420, the 18th year of the Yongle reign of the Ming Dynasty, the hexagonal Xili Pavilion to the northwest of the pillar was originally located in the Honglu Court responsible for the rites of the Ming and Qing Dynasties. Due to acts of devastation carried out by the Eight - Power Allied Force in 1900, Honglu Court behind the eastern side of Tian'anmen was burned to the ground, leaving just Xili Pavilion. In the past, officials and foreign diplomatic envoys coming to court the emperor had to go to Xili Pavilion first to learn the relevant rites. The pavilion was moved into Zhongshan Park in 1915.

Key Words & Expressions

1. Xili Pavilion 习礼亭
2. hexagonal 六角形的
3. Honglu Court 鸿胪寺
4. foreign diplomatic envoy 外国使节

Altar to the God of Land and Grain & Zhongshan Hall
社稷坛和中山堂

The major architectural item in Zhongshan Park, the Altar to the God of Land and Grain, is located on the central axle. The name of the altar in Chinese represents land and grain, and it was used to offer sacrifices to the God of Land and Grain by the emperor. The three-layered altar symbolizes the land, with the upper layer 16 meters long, the middle 16.8 meters and the lower 17.8 meters long. Five colors of soil; yellow, green, white, red and black, were used to pave the upper layer. The soil was said to be tributes paid nationwide, representing the emperor's ownership of the entire nation. According to the Taoist theory of *Yin* and *Yang*, the five elements of gold, wood, water, fire and soil are the basis for everything. There is also a square stone pillar erected in the middle of the altar, bespeaking the eternity of imperial power. It was removed in 1950. The ancient Chinese idolized the God of Land and Grain, and the emperor offered sacrifices every February and August, praying for a bumper harvest.

If there were fires, floods, and a solar eclipse or if the army was dispatched, ceremonies also took place here. Hence, *Sheji* became the symbol of the nation. With red walls surrounding it, the altar has one entrance on each side, built at the order of the emperor.

Zhongshan Hall, to the north of the altar, was the resting place of the emperor. On rainy days, temporary sacrificial tables would be installed in the hall for the emperor to offer sacrifices. With a stone base, the five-room-wide and three-room-deep wooden hall was built in 1425, the first year of Hongxi reign of the Ming Dynasty. After the death of Sun Yat-sen in 1925, his casket was once kept here. In honor of the great man, the hall was renamed Zhongshan Hall in 1928. Its original style of the early Ming Dynasty was well preserved, despite later renovations.

Key Words & Expressions

1. Altar to the God of Land and Grain 社稷坛
2. tributes 贡物
3. idolize 崇拜
4. bumper harvest 丰收
5. solar eclipse 日食
6. Zhongshan Hall 中山堂

Lantingbei Pavilion 兰亭碑亭

Originally built as one of the 40 scenes in Yuanming Park, Lantingbei Pavilion consists of one tablet and eight stone pillars, known as the Lanting tablet and eight pillars. After the destruction of Yuanming Park, the Lanting tablet was moved into Zhongshan Park in 1917, and the eight pillars into the Summer Palace. On the obverse side of the stone tablet was inscribed a pattern of flowing water along Lanting Pavilion, and on the reverse is a poem by Emperor Qianlong of the Qing Dynasty. Copies of the Lanting poem by famous calligraphers were inscribed on the eight pillars. It was not until early 1971 that the eight pillars were moved from the Summer Palace into the octagonal Lantingbei Pavilion of Zhongshan Park, restoring it to its original state.

Key Words & Expressions

1. Lantingbei Pavilion 兰亭碑亭
2. calligrapher 书法家
3. octagonal 八边形的

Orchid Pavilion and Flower Exhibition 唐花坞与花展

Located in the southwest of Zhongshan

Park, the swallow - wing - shaped Orchid Pavilion is a double - eaved octagonal pavilion with glass greenhouses on both sides. As a matter of fact, the Orchid Pavilion itself is a greenhouse too. With red pillars and blue eaves, the small greenhouse looks rather lovely. An over two - meter - high stone is installed in the center of the pond with a big fountain, in which goldfish swim freely. Varieties of famous flowers are on display, including 39 types of tulips donated by the Netherlands in 1977. Tulip exhibitions are held here each year, and themed flower exhibitions frequently take place.

Key Words & Expressions

1. Orchid Pavilion 唐花坞
2. tulip 郁金香
3. themed flower exhibitions 专题花展

Working People's Cultural Palace
劳动人民文化宫

History 演变

Originally the Royal Ancestral Temple,

the Working People' s Cultural Palace to the east of the Forbidden City, once hosted ceremonies during important festivals, including the emperor's wedding and enthronement, the dispatch and withdrawal of the army. Built in 1420, the 18th year of Yongle reign of the Ming Dynasty, after several renovations it covers an area of 140,000 sq meters. With three enclosing walls, the palace is rectangular in shape. As one of the best - preserved ancient complex, it opened to the public as Heping (Peace) Park in 1942 and became a branch of the Palace Museum in 1928. It was given its current name on May 1, 1950, and many new entertainment areas were added, including an open - air theatre, cinema, and gymnasium for children, mini theatre and a library. It' s indeed a paradise for people' s cultural activities. A book market, often held here during spring and autumn, was relocated to the Park of the Temple of Earth in 2002.

Key Words & Expressions

1. Working People's Cultural Palace
   劳动人民文化宫
2. enthronement 登基
3. Palace Museum 故宫博物院

4. open－air theatre 露天剧场
5. gymnasium 体育场
6. relocate 挪地方

Three Halls and Their Main Functions
三大殿及其作用

The Royal Ancestral Temple is mainly comprised of the three halls. The double－eaved front sacrificial hall with three white marble bases and stone fences is 11 rooms wide and four rooms deep. Memorial tablets of past emperors and empresses were kept here in the hall, with an altar in the front. The two side halls served to hold the spirit tablets of the royal family and officials displaying outstanding performances. The nine－room middle hall, or residential hall, was used to hold empresses' memorial tablets of the Qing Dynasty, and its two side rooms served to stock the sacrificial vessels, and the nine－room rear hall served to keep the tablets of emperors and empresses before the founding of the Qing Dynasty. Set in the shadows of lush pine and green cypress, the three halls appear mysterious and splendid.

Key Words & Expressions

1. sacrificial hall 祭殿

2. residential hall 寝宫
3. memorial tablet 牌位
4. sacrificial vessel 祭器
5. rear hall 后殿
6. lush 青葱的

Chinese Serial Bells 中华和钟

The Chinese serial bells were made on the basis of the Zenghou Yi bell of 2,400 years ago in November 1999, to celebrate the advent of the new century. On the first day of the new century, President Jiang Zemin first struck the bells in the Royal Ancestral Temple. They were kept in the temple for tourists to see.

Made up of 108 bells, the three-layer Chinese Serial Bells are 3.8 meters high, 21 meters wide and weigh 17 tons. The 34 bells in the upper layer represent the 32 provinces, autonomous regions and municipalities directly under the Central Government, and Hong Kong SAR and Macao SAR. The 56 bells in the middle represent China's 56 nationalities. In the lower layer the 16 bells in the middle out of 18 bells symbolize the 16 historic periods of the Chinese people, and the two side bells symbolize Peace and Development world-wide. On the 320-kg central bell, Zhonghua Hezhong, Wannian Yongbao (Chinese serial bells last forever), is inscribed in eight gilded characters written by Jiang Zemin. The serial bells express the Chinese people's best wishes for unity and prosperity of the nation and world peace and development in the new century.

Key Words & Expressions

1. Chinese serial bell 中华和钟
2. Hong Kong SAR 香港特别行政区
3. prosperity 繁荣

The Great Hall of the People
人民大会堂

Introduction 简介

Meetings of the National People's Congress to discuss national affairs are usually held in the Great Hall of the People, and it is also used for important political and cultural activities of national leaders and the people. Leaders of the Party and the nation receive foreign leaders and hold important international meetings here to promote friendship and world peace.

Wholly designed by Chinese, construction of the hall commenced in October 1958, and completed the following August. It is 336 meters long from south to north, and 206 meters wide from east to west. The highest point in the center reaches 46.5 meters; it covers an area of 171,800 sq meters, the tallest building on Tian'anmen Square.

It consists of a huge 10,000-seat auditorium, northern banquet hall and the southern office buildings of the standing committee. There are more than 300 meeting rooms, lounges and offices, satisfying the needs of meetings and conferences.

Key Words & Expressions

1. National People's Congress
   全国人民代表大会
2. auditorium 礼堂
3. banquet hall 宴会大厅
4. consist of 由…组成

Colonnade 廊柱

There are 134 colonnades in the Great Hall of the People. Facing east, the main entrance is 83 meters wide. On the five-meter-high steps are 12 colonnades of reinforced concrete paved with natural marble. The colonnades are so big that four people can only just get their arms around it. Distances between the colonnades vary, ranging from 10.3 meters, 8.2 meters and 7.15 meters to 7 meters. The distance between the inner cores are 9 meters between the middle two, and 7 meters between the others. As the two colonnades in the middle appear somewhat closer than the others do, the architect paid special treatment to them while laying the marble paving. This clever treatment avoided pulling down the already built colonnades, saving much manpower and resources.

Key Words & Expressions

1. colonnade 廊柱
2. reinforced concrete 钢筋混凝土
3. inner core 内芯
4. architect 建筑师
5. manpower 人力

Central Multifunctional Hall
中央大厅

Upon entering the east gate, the central multifunctional hall will greet you. Covering an area of 3, 600 sq meters, it is 76 meters long from north to south, 48 meters deep and

16 meters high. Its 20 internal square pillars and flooring are all paved with marble. The central hall is where entertainment and festive activities and ceremonies to welcome foreign leaders are held, and where people attending conferences can rest.

Key Words & Expressions

1. multifunctional hall 多功能大厅
2. internal 内部的
3. festive 欢庆的

10,000 - seat Auditorium

万人大礼堂

With out any pillar to support it, the 10,000 - seat auditorium is the main architectural feature of the Great Hall of the People. The auditorium is 76 meters wide, 60 meters long and 32 meters high and its three floors of seats successively ascend. There are 3,693 seats on the first floor, 3,515 seats on the second, 2, 518 seats the third floor and 300 - 500 seats on the rostrum, and people seated anywhere in the fan - shaped auditorium can see the rostrum. On the ceiling are 500 lamps, resembling stars shining in the sky when lit.

Key Words & Expressions

1. ascend 上升
2. successively 接连着
3. rostrum 主席台
4. resemble 像

Banqueting Hall 宴会大厅

Grand banquets and large receptions hosted by leaders of the Party and the nation are held in the northern banqueting hall on the second floor. Covering an area of over 7, 000 sq meters, the 102 - meter - long, 76 - meter - wide and 15 - meter - high hall can cater for 5, 000 people at a seat - down banquet, or parties for 10, 000 people. Kitchens at its eastern and western sides can provide both Chinese and Western food. The huge banqueting hall has no pillars to support it; another excellent piece of architecture. Colorful caisson on the ceiling depict unique ethnic characteristics.

Key Words & Expressions

1. reception 招待会
2. caisson 藻井
3. depict 体现,描述
4. ethnic 种族的

Provincial Halls 各省厅

Among the 300 meeting halls, lounges and offices, 34 of them are rather special, representing the provinces, autonomous regions and municipalities directly under the central government, Hong Kong SAR and Macao SAR. Bearing the particular name of the place it represents, the various halls are decorated by unique handicrafts and ornaments with particular ethnic features. These include a famous cork carving in Fujian Hall, bamboo handicrafts in Sichuan Hall, terracotta warriors and horses in Shanxi Hall and a wool embroidered picture of a night scene of Victoria Harbor in Hong Kong Hall displaying not only local culture, but also their different economic power.

Key Words & Expressions

1. decorate 装饰
2. handicraft 手工艺品
3. ornament 装饰品
4. bamboo 竹子
5. terracotta warriors and horses 兵马俑
6. Victoria Harbor 维多利亚港

Museum of Chinese History and Museum of Chinese Revolution
中国历史博物馆与中国革命博物馆

The Museum of Chinese History and Museum of Chinese Revolution, closely connected with each other, was one of 10 constructions built on the 10th anniversary of the founding of PRC. Covering an area of 69, 000 sq meters, it is 313 meters long and 149 meters wide.

Museum of Chinese History
中国历史博物馆

As the most well known museum of history, the Museum of Chinese History is the one with the largest collection of historic relics and most profound study in this field, displaying several thousand years of culture. Occupying an area of 61, 000 sq meters, the 80 - year - old museum was moved to the present location in 1959.

The exhibition of historical relics consists of three parts, in the order of the development of our ancient history. Beginning from primitive society, the first part exhibits a myriad of precious cultural relics from 1.7 million years ago to approximately 4, 000 years ago. The second part exhibiting the slave society covers the history of the Xia, Shang and Zhou Dynasties and the Spring and Autumn Period (2, 100 B.C – 476B.C) . The third part displays feudal society(475 B.C – 1840 A.D) and shows the general trend of the society, from division to ultimate union. The massive exhibition of historical relics, documents, pictures and models indicates systematically and scientifically the past 5, 000 – year civilization of the Chinese people. It is an ideal place to learn about Chinese history, and for youth to receive a patriotic education.

The rare collection exhibition of the museum focuses on major relics of general history. An exhibition of calligraphy by modern celebrities and an exhibition of life in the Tang Dynasty are being displayed.

Key Words & Expressions

1. historic relics 历史文物
2. display 展示
3. primitive society 原始社会
4. myriad 无数的

5. approximately 大约
6. feudal society 封建社会
7. ultimate 最终的
8. massive 大量的

Museum of Chinese Revolution
中国革命博物馆

The most famous one of its kind, the Museum of Chinese Revolution is located to the east of Tian'anmen Square. Covering an area of 8,000 sq meters, it was built in 1959. A national museum displaying the development of a socialist country, it has collected relics since the Opium War in 1840. It involves the propagation of Marxism and Mao Zedong Thought, and the education of revolutionary tradition.

It boasts two floors of exhibition rooms, covering an area of 4,000 sq meters each. In addition, there are two theme halls holding exhibitions of the two revolutionary periods before and after 1919. The exhibition hall of democratic revolution(1840 - 1919) is divided into 8 parts, the Opium War, Taipingtianguo Revolution, Sino - French War and Sino - Japanese War, Russian Invasion, Political Reform of 1898, the Boxers' Movement,

Revolution of 1911 and the New Dawn. Covering an area of 1,300 sq meters, the hall displays nearly 1,000 relics, pictures and material objects, revealing the solemn and stirring history of struggle of the Chinese people before the founding of the Chinese Communist Party. The exhibition hall of the new democratic revolution (1919 - 1949) is divided into five parts: the founding of the Chinese Communist Party, the first and second Civil Wars, the War of Resistance against Japanese Aggression and the third Civil War. The 4,000-sq-meter hall exhibits 4, 000 relics, objects and pictures, displaying the entire process of the Chinese people's struggle, under the guidance of the Chinese Communist Party, against imperialism, feudalism and bureaucratic capitalism, and the founding of the PRC.

Home to a collection of over 100, 000 cultural relics and 200,000 books, the museum is the important place for the people to learn and research the history of Chinese revolution and receive an education of revolutionary tradition.

Due to internal repairs, the exhibition of old and new democratic revolution in the museum has been replaced by the "I Love You,

China: Exhibition of China' s National Flag, National Emblem and National Anthem" and a Photographic Exhibition depicting the cities of Beijing, Tianjing, Shanghai and Chongqing, a new way for tourists to learn the history of the Chinese Revolution.

Key Words & Expressions

1. socialist country 社会主义国家
2. propagation 宣传
3. Marxism 马列主义
4. Mao Zedong Thought 毛泽东思想
5. Taipingtianguo Revolution
   太平天国革命运动
6. Sino-French War 中法战争
7. Russian Invasion 沙俄对中国的侵略
8. Political Reform of 1898 戊戌变法
9. Sino-Japanese War 中日战争
10. Revolution of 1911 辛亥革命
11. third Civil War 第三次国内革命战争
12. bureaucratic capitalism 官僚资本主义
13. national emblem 国徽

Jingshan Park

景 山

Tour Route
参观路线

South Gate—(eastward) Suicide place of Emperor Chongzhen—Guanmiao (viewing excellence) Pavilion — Zhoushang Pavilion — Wanchun (myriads of springs) Pavilion — (westward) Fulan Pavilion—Jifang Pavilion— (eastward down the mountain) Qiwang Tower—out of the south gate.

Location and Main Architecture
景山的地理位置及主要建筑

Jingshan Park is located on the central axle of Beijing City, beyond the north gate of the Forbidden City. The central axle runs from Yongdingmen Gate, through Qianmen Gate, Tian'anmen Gate, the Forbidden City and Wanchun Pavilion, and finally reaches Di'anmen Gate, the Drum Tower and the Bell Tower. Jingshan Park was originally built for the exclusive use of the emperors during the Yuan, Ming and Qing Dynasties. On top of each of the rolling hills are pavilions in diverse styles, rendering the hills more dimly discernable as a barrier to the north of the Forbidden City. The ancient green pines and strong cypress, plus peony blossom abounding with butterflies provide a glamorous scene. In the Ming Dynasty, the then called Wansui Mountain abounded in lush trees, flocks of cranes and cavorting deer. At the foot of the mountain was once Baiguo Orchard, amass with flowers and fruit. Jingshan Mountain was where the emperors hiked, feasted, appreciated flowers and practiced archery. It was opened to the public in 1928, the 17th year of the Republic of China. After the founding of the PRC, it became park for ordinary citizens. The middle Ridge of Jingshan Mountain is 44.1 meters high, and used to be the apex of Beijing City. The mountain demonstrated the supremacy of imperial power and defended the Forbidden City, and from it you can view the panorama of Beijing. From east to west, there are five ridges, on each was built a glazed – tile pavilion. Wanchun Pavilion on the highest peak is the largest, with Zhoushang Pavilion and Guanmiao Pavilion standing at the eastern sides in attendance and Fulan Pavilion and Jifang Pavilion at the western sides. The four pavilions descended in height in symmetry. There was an old sophora on eastern Jingshan Mountain, where Emperor Zhu youjian of Chongzhen reign hanged himself when Li Zicheng took Beijing with peasant uprising. It is now an exhibition hall. Shouhuang Hall and Guande Hall have been transformed into the Beijing Children's Palace and its library, a place where children study, play and conduct scientific activities.

Key Words & Expressions

1. Drum Tower 鼓楼
2. Bell Tower 钟楼
3. rolling 起伏的
4. Baiguo Orchard 百果园
5. peony 牡丹
6. crane 鹤
7. cavort 欢跳
8. hike 远足
9. apex 顶点
10. panorama 全景

Formation and Origin of the Name
景山的形成及其名称的由来

The formation of Jingshan Mountain has much to do with the construction of Beijing and the emperors of the Yuan, Ming and Qing Dynasties. There was just a mass of wilderness here 800 years ago. During the reign of the Jin Period, the present Beihai was canalized in the construction of Daning Palace, leaving an earthen hummock. Later, in the 13th century, Emperor Kublai Khan of the Yuan Dynasty ordered the building of the capital Dadu in Beijing. Located at the very center was a park for the amusement of the emperor. Having long been covered by exuberant grasses, the original earth hummock was called Qingshan Mountain, the predecessor of the present Jingshan Mountain.

During construction of the Forbidden City in 1416, workers left silt, dust and soil on the original hummock, which gradually formed into the five ridges. Since it was a natural screen defending the Forbidden City, it was regarded as the guarding mountain of the Ming and Qing Dynasties. It was said that Emperor Zhu Di once stocked coal here, so Jingshan Mountain was also called Coal Mountain.

Renamed Jingshan Mountain in 1655, the 12th year of Shunzhi Reign of Qing Dynasty, it was used as a place to hold sacrificial activities. Jing in Chinese means high. In one poem of the Book of Songs, it is written that, having mounted Jingshan Mountain in the capital of the Shang Dynasty, the people appreciated the beautiful scenery while praising the exuberance of the pine and cypress. The entire poem spoke highly of Emperor Wuding of the Shang Dynasty, who saved the nation from disaster and brought it to prosperity once again. The people then built an ancestral temple for him with pine and cypresses on the mountain to show respect to him. At the beginning of the Qing Dynasty, Emperor Fu Lin of Shunzhi reign renamed Wansui Mountain as Jingshan Mountain, wishing for lasting stability and durable peace.

Key Words & Expressions

1. wilderness 荒郊野地
2. canalize 开凿运河
3. hummock 圆丘
4. Kublai Khan 忽必烈
5. exuberant 繁茂的
6. silt 淤泥
7. Coal Mountain 煤山
8. Book of Songs 诗经
9. ancestral temple 宗庙
10. durable 持久的

Qiwang Tower 绮望楼

Entering Beishangmen Gate, the main south gate opposite the Gate of Military

Prowess of the Forbidden City, Qiwang Tower greets visitors. Along the mountain, the tower looks quite delicate. Originally, Emperor Qianlong kept the memorial tablet of Confucius here. The rooms beside Beishangmen Gate were the study for offspring of the department of internal affairs. They are now used as halls to hold art exhibitions of paintings, ceramics and calligraphies. Colorful flowers can be seen along the road up the mountain behind the tower.

Key Words & Expressions

1. Confucius 孔夫子
2. offspring 后代
3. department of internal affairs 内务府
4. ceramics 陶瓷

Five Pavilions
景山上的五亭

The above – mentioned five pavilions on the five ridges of Jingshan Mountain were built in 1751, the 15th year of the Emperor Qianlong' s reign. Fulan Pavilion to the west and Zhoushang Pavilion to the east of Wanchun Pavilion on the middle ridge, the summit of Jingshan Mountain, are in symmetry with the other two double - eaved round pavilions with blue tiles. The eastern one is called Guanmiao Pavilion and the western one Jifang Pavilion. There is bronze statue in each of the five pavilions, representing the five kinds of tastes. Hence, the five statues of gods are also called Five - Taste God. The bronze statues in the four pavilions, excepting the middle one, were plundered by the Eight - Power Allied Force in 1900, and the left arm of the statue in Wanchun Pavilion was cut off. Tourists on Jingshan Mountain can overlook the panorama of Beijing.

Key Words & Expressions

1. summit 顶点
2. bronze statue 铜像
3. Five - Taste God 五味神
4. plunder 抢劫
5. overlook 俯瞰

A Bird's Eye View of Beijing from Wanchun Pavilion 万春亭上鸟瞰京城

The east and west sides can access visitors to the middle ridge. Standing in Wanchun Pavilion, tourists can fully enjoy the grand scene of the entire mountain.

Looking north, you can see Di'anmen Street. The Drum Tower to the north of the street looks like a huge diamond inlaid on a jade belt. Several new buildings have been erected along both sides of the street closer to Jingshan Mountain. The buildings with green glazed tiles are in harmony with the palaces with yellow glazed tiles.

The lovely scenery of Beihai Park to the southwest of Jingshan Mountain makes you feel as if you are in south China. Shishahai Park is just one road away from Beihai Park. Along the lovely mountain and beside the clear water, tourists meander around the lake, where a few boats can be found, and flocks of doves fly around the White Pagoda. To the south of Wanchun Pavilion, you can get a bird' s eye view of the layout of Beijing and the central axle, on which are located many important classic architectural structures. The Working People' s Cultural Palace and Zhongshan Park are situated at the two sides of the axle. In the middle, the glazed – tile roofs of palaces in the Forbidden City shine in the sun, "flowing" in a sea of green pines and cypresses. Tian' anmen Square lies in front of the Forbidden City, between the Tian'anmen and Qianmen Gates.

A cluster of modern hotels, standing tall in the rays of the morning sunshine on Wangfujing Commercial Street to the east of the mountain, provides us with yet another beautiful scene of the modern city.

Key Words & Expressions

1. a bird's eye view 鸟瞰
2. inlay 镶嵌
3. meander 漫步
4. dove 鸽子
5. White Pagoda 白塔
6. cluster 串,丛

Suicide Place of Emperor Chongzhen of the Ming Dynasty 明崇祯帝自缢处

On a hill to the east of Guanmiao Pavilion, you can see a sophora enclosed by fences. This is the spot where the last emperor of the Ming Dynasty hanged himself. The original tree, bound in chains, was called the "guilty sophora". When the Eight-Power Allied Forces invaded Beijing, the chains were removed. Later, people built walls around the tree and erected a stele inscribed, "Where the last emperor of the Ming Dynasty died". However, all these were destroyed in the Cultural Revolution, and even the sophora was cut down. The tree we see today was planted at a later date.

Emperor Chongzhen's suicide was inevitable. On March 17, 1644, Li Zicheng, leading a group of rebels, captured Beijing and the army surrendered. The next day, the stationed army of Fuchengmen Gate and Xibianmen Gate welcomed the rebels. The emperor intended to escape via the south gate of the

Forbidden City, but in vain, and had to return to the palace. He then killed the princesses and forced the empress to commit suicide. The next morning the emperor, in white robe and wearing shoes belonging to eunuch Wang Cheng'en, climbed up Jingshan Mountain. Lingering for a moment, the emperor hanged himself on the sophora. It was said that he sighed before untying his belt and hanging himself, saying, "I treated them rather well, but nobody came to die with me." The fame of the mountain owes much to the suicide of the emperor. People in the reign of Jiaqing of the Qing Dynasty wrote poems to mourn the emperor. It said that trees abound on the green mountain; where the soul of the emperor cried sadly.

Key Words & Expressions

1. sophora 槐树
2. inevitable 无法避免的
3. surrender 投降
4. in vain 失败
5. commit suicide 自杀
6. owe …to 因…而
7. mourn 悼念

Shouhuang Hall and Guande Hall
寿皇殿和观德堂

The original Shouhuang Hall built in the Ming Dynasty was moved to the present location in 1749 and extended. The extended architecture is comprised of the main hall, right and left halls, east and west attached halls and kitchens, stele pavilion and well pavilion. There is a halbert gate in front of the nine rooms of the main hall, coupled with the glazed chamber and stone lions. The original altar of Emperor Kangxi was used to worship portraits of royal ancestors, and to store the caskets of the emperors since the time of Emperor Shunzhi. Today, it is the Beijing Children's Palace and a paradise for children.

The Guande Hall to the east of Shouhuang Hall was used by the royal family to exercise during the Ming Dynasty, and later for the storage of emperors' caskets.

Key Words & Expressions

1. be comprised of 由…组成
2. attached hall 配殿

3. stele pavilion 碑亭
4. halbert gate 戟门

Guanyu Temple
关帝庙

Guanyu Temple behind Jingshan Mountain served as a place to worship the statue of Guanyu, a general of the kingdom Shu in the Three Kingdoms Period. Prior to the Song Dynasty, Guanyu was not so well known. In the Ming Dynasty, he was proclaimed the Martial Saint, similar to Confucius. Ordinary citizens regarded him as a God capable of warding off evil, protecting merchants, curing diseases and making people rich. Therefore everyone, old or young, idolized him and worshiped him in temples. Due to his fidelity to the king, Guanyu was used by the rulers to moralize the people and maintain the feudal reign. Even in the Qing Dynasty, Guanyu was worshipped as the god of the nation protection by the emperor. The emperor also used Guanyu Temple in an attempt to maintain social stability and peace. Accordingly, the temple was officially called the temple of fidelity.

Key Words & Expressions

1. Three Kingdoms Period 三国时期
2. proclaim 宣布
3. Martial Saint 武圣人
4. temple of fidelity 护国忠义庙

Jingshan Mountain and Peking University 景山与北京大学

Decades ago, Jingshan Mountain was utilized by Peking University, when its east faced directly onto Mashenmiao Street. Most of the boys of the school of arts, science and law resided in the west chamber, west of Mashenmiao, and girls in new buildings along the lane of the Prince Song's Residence. During the period of the Republic of China, Jingshan Mountain was opened to the public as Jingshan Park. After the founding of the PRC, it was given special protection as an important cultural relic by the Beijing Municipality. Several renovations were done and roads built. Many fruit trees and flowers were planted, rendering it one of the city' s most popular parks.

Key Words & Expressions

1. Prince Song's Residence 嵩公府
2. Republic of China 中华民国

Beihai Park

北海

Tour Route
参观路线

The entire tour around Beihai Park can be divided into two parts:

1) Qiongdao Island Scenic Area: the south gate—Tuancheng (round city)—(across Yong' an Bridge) Yong' an Temple — the White Pagoda — (downhill from the northwest) Yuexin Hall— Qingxiao Tower—Yuegu Tower — the Bronze Dew Plate — the Qiongdaochunyin Stele.

2) Scenes along Beihai: the west gate (east or north gate is also ideal) —the drill

ground tablet—the stone tablet of the Wanfo (10,000 - Buddha) Tower—Five Dragon Pavilion — Iron Screen Wall — Nine Dragon Screen — Studio of Rested Heart — Tianwang (heavenly king) Hall— Silkworm Altar—the north gate—Pleasure Boat Chamber— Haopu Chamber—the east gate

Introduction
概 况

Beihai Park is 500 meters to the west of the north gate of the Forbidden City. The original royal park was out of bounds to ordinary citizens. It covers an area of over 700,000 sq meters, and more than half is water. Since the Liao Dynasty, the Jin, Yuan, Ming and Qing Dynasties built royal parks here. The lake and marsh in the Liao Dynasty was built into Xanadu, the highest palace serving as a dressing table for Empress Dowager Xiao. Later in the Jin Dynasty, Qionghua (Jade Flower) Island, Yaoguang Hall and Guanghan Hall were constructed, and the Taihu stone of the Gen Mountain in the Song Dynasty was moved from Kaifeng, Henan. Xanadu was built into Daning Palace on the outskirts of the capital of the Jin Dynasty in 1179. Emperor Kublai Khan of the Yuan Dynasty then ordered the construction the new capital Dadu, surrounding Qionghua (Jade Flower) Island (renamed Wanshou Mountain) and Taiye Pool. Taiye Pool was cut into two parts, and the lake dug during the Ming Dynasty and Beihai, Zhonghai and Nanhai came into being. Many halls, chambers and pavilions were built successively along its banks during the Ming and Qing Dynasties. A Tibetan-style white pagoda was built on the original site of Guanghan Hall, and Wanshou Mountain renamed White Pagoda Mountain in 1651, the 8th year of Shunzhi reign. The original Taiye Pool and Qionghua (Jade Flower) Island were constructed into the largest and most beautiful royal park. When the Eight-Power Allied Force invaded Beijing in 1900, Beihai Park was the base for the headquarters of Japan, France and Russia, and almost reduced to ashes. Two years later, Empress Dowager Cixi renovated the park as a residence for herself. It remained closed to the public until

1925, marking an end of its history as imperial park.

Key Words & Expressions

1. Bronze Dew Plate 铜仙人承露盘
2. Iron Screen Wall 铁影壁
3. Nine Dragon Screen 九龙壁
4. Studio of Rested Heart 静心斋
5. Silkworm Altar 先蚕坛
6. Pleasure Boat Chamber 画舫斋
7. reduced to ashes 化为灰烬
8. Empress Dowager 太后

Round City
团 城

General Survey 简介

Outside the south gate of Beihai Park is an ancient round garden architecture, over 800 years old. It was an islet to the south of Qionghua (Jade Flower) Island in the Liao Dynasty and part of Daning Palace in the Jin Dynasty. When constructing the capital Dadu around Taiye Pool, Kublai Khan ordered people to build Yitian Hall on the original site of the Jin Dynasty and a stone city on a circular platform. Later during Yongle reign in the Ming Dynasty, brick walls were built around the island and Yitian Hall reconstructed. It was renamed as Chengguang (receiving light) Hall in 1417 and Qianguang Hall in 1552. Large – scale renovation was done on the round city after its destruction due to an earthquake in 1669, the 8th year of Kangxi reign. Restoration of Qianguang Hall was completed in 1746, when it was then called Chengguang Hall.

A royal park for emperors, the round city is 276 meters in circumference, surrounded by a 4.6 – meter – high wall, covering an area of 4, 550 sq meters. Comprising primarily of Chengguang Hall and Jade Urn Pavilion, the round city appears pretty, delicate, lovely and unique among ancient garden structures. Facing water on two of its sides, the round city shines like a pearl embedded in a jade plate. There are two gates on its east and west sides; the eastern one is Zhaojing Gate, and the western is Yanxiang Gate. The latter was destroyed in 1900 when the Eight – Power Allied Force invaded Beijing City, and reconstructed in 1953. Ordered by the late Prime Minster

Zhou Enlai, stairs were built on the northern side so tourists can pay visits to the round city directly from Beihai Park. Arts and craft exhibitions are often held here.

Key Words & Expressions

1. islet 小岛
2. round city 团城
3. Jade Urn Pavilion 玉瓮亭
4. arts and craft exhibitions
   工艺美术展览

Chengguang Hall 承光殿

Built on an octagonal terrace, the double-eaved Chengguang Hall is an octagonal hall with 12 rooms. The beautiful single-eaved verandas and unique-styled yellow tiles are a rare sight in ancient architecture. Entering the hall, visitors will find handwriting by Emperor Xianfeng of the Qing Dynasty on four huge pillars, coupled with a horizontal inscribed board handwritten by Empress Dowager Cixi. In the center-right of the hall is a seated statue of Sakyamuni. Carved from a single piece of white jade, the 1.5-meter-high immaculate statue indicates the excellence of China's jade carving techniques. The kasaya worn by Sakyamuni is embedded with small red and green gems, items of rare treasure. The jade Buddha statue was said to have been presented to Cixi by the Beijing monk Ming Kuan, who begged alms in Burma in 1897. Cixi then placed it in the Chengguang Hall of the round city. There is a scar caused by knife on the left arm of the statue, made during the invasion of the Eight - Power Allied Force in 1900.

Key Words & Expressions

1. terrace 台基
2. veranda 抱厦
3. horizontal 水平的
4. Sakyamuni 释迦牟尼
5. kasaya 袈裟
6. Burma 缅甸
7. beg alms 募化

"Shade Marquis" 遮荫侯

There is a pine standing tall, straight and verdant to the east of Chengguang Hall, planted in the Jin Dynasty. Emperor Qianlong of the Qing Dynasty granted it the title "Shade Marquis". The 800 - year - old pine is counted as a treasure of ancient trees.

Jade Urn Pavilion 玉瓮亭

In the Jade Urn Pavilion in front of Chengguang Hall is a jade urn displayed on a white marble lotus pedestal, carved from of a single piece of jet. The urn is 0.7 meter high, 1.5 meters in diameter, 5 meters in circumference and weighs 3, 500 kg. Fancy decorative patterns of fish, dragons and sea animals frolicking in waves carved on the surface reveal exquisite craftsmanship. It was believed to be a wine vessel used by Kublai Khan during banquets with officials in 1265, and stored in Guanghan Hall on top of the White Pagoda. With the demolition of Guanghan Hall in the Ming Dynasty, the urn fell into the hands of Taoist priests belonging to Zhenwu Temple, outside Xihua Gate. The Taoist priests first used it to hold vegetables, before putting it in the hall as a treasure. Emperor Qianlong bought it off them for 1, 000 – liang of silver, and had the pavilion built to house it in 1749. Considering the original name boorish, the emperor renamed it Jade Urn and had the Ode to the Jade Urn (which he composed) inscribed on the interior of the urn. Poems by members of the Imperial Academy can also be seen on the square pillars at the corners of the pavilion. The jet may have originated from Minshan Mountain in west Sichuan, which was called Jade Mountain.

Key Words & Expressions

1. Shade Marquis 遮荫侯
2. lotus pedestal 莲座
3. jet 墨玉
4. Taoist priest 道士
5. boorish 粗鄙的
6. Imperial Academy 翰林院

Qionghua (Jade Flower) Island 琼华岛

Qionghua Island 琼华岛

Located in the southeast corner of the waters of Beihai, Qionghua (Jade Flower) Island was built as part of Xanadu in the Liao Dynasty, but renamed Qionghua (Jade Flower) Island as part of the Wanning Palace in the Jin Dynasty. It was called Wanshou (Longevity) Mountain in the Yuan Dynasty and White Pagoda Mountain in the Qing Dynasty. It is 45 meters high and 900 meters in circumference. Despite the weathering of hundreds of years, it still appears like a fabulous mirage from a fairy tale. Lying on the central axle of the White Pagoda, the island projects the White Pagoda, a symbol of supreme imperial power. Moved from the imperial garden of the Northern Song Dynasty, Taihu stones are scattered about on the island, forming hills, cliffs, terraces and rockeries. Yong'an Temple is situated in the south, with Jianchun Pavilion, Guyi Chamber, Kanhua (painting view) corridor and Jiaocui Pavilion in the east and other chambers in the north and west. Rockeries are formed here and there, enhancing the beauty of the island. There are two grotesque stones to the north of Dharma Hall, with two characters---Kunlun and three poems in the handwriting of Emperor Qianlong. Stone stairs and roads stretch to the four sides of the island, and stone bridges, setting off the enchanting beauty of the scene, connect the eastern and southern sides.

Key Words & Expressions

1. fabulous 难以置信的
2. enhance 提高
3. grotesque 奇特的

4. enchanting 迷人的
5. set off 交相辉映

Yong'an Temple 永安寺

Connected with the round city by Yong' an Bridge (a white marble bridge built in the 13th century), Yong'an Temple is situated in the south of Qionghua (Jade Flower) Island. There is an arch on the southern and northern ends of Yong' an Bridge, the northern one called Coiling Clouds, and the southern one Amassing Green, stationed by a pair of stone lions. Yong' an Temple was built on the site of Renzhi Hall, Jiefu Hall and Yanhe Hall of the Ming Dynasty in 1651. Originally named White Pagoda Temple, Yong' an Temple received its current name in 1743, the 8th year of Emperor Qianlong's reign. The temple and the White Pagoda consists in the central axle of the island. Dharma Hall, Zhengjue Hall, Pu' an Hall and Shanyin Hall were built along the mountain in an ascending order. Together with the White Pagoda, they formed a complete Tibetan lamasery of the Yellow Hat Lamaism.

Key Words & Expressions

1. arch 牌坊

2. Coiling Clouds 堆云
3. Amassing Green 积翠
4. Dharma Hall 法轮殿
5. lamasery 喇嘛寺庙
6. Yellow Hat Lamaism 黄教

White Pagoda 白塔

On top of Qionghua (Jade Flower) Island, the White Pagoda is the most prominent architecture on the island. First built in 1651, the 8th year of Shunzhi reign, it was restored twice after earthquakes in the reign of Kangxi and Yongzheng. After the founding of the People's Republic of China, several renovations finally restored it to its original style.

A Lamaism pagoda, the vase - shaped White Pagoda on a brick pedestal is 35.9 meters in height. Fourteen bronze bells hang from its bronze canopy, on top of which is a gilt ball like a flame. The glazed - tiled Shanyin Hall to its south houses a bronze statue of Bodhisattva Manjusri in the center, and other Buddha images with thousand of hands and eyes carved on walls. Annual Buddhist ceremonies were held there on the 25th day of the 10th lunar month. Lamps from the foot of the mountain to the top of the pagoda were lit, like stars in the sky. Lamas usually piped and drummed till late in the night, praying for happiness and auspices. There were five poles to the north of the pagoda, in case of an enemy attack. During emergencies, a dragon flag would be raised in the daytime and lanterns lit at night. The flags varied in colors according to their different directions, blue for the east, white for the west, red for the south, black for the north and yellow for the inner city. If the enemy attacked from the eastern and western sides in the daytime, blue and white dragon flags would be raised. Seeing the signal, the eight－banner army would gather immediately to fight against the enemy.

Key Words & Expressions

1. prominent 突出的
2. canopy 伞盖
3. Bodhisattva Manjusri 文殊菩萨
4. auspice 吉祥
5. eight－banner army 八旗兵

Yuexin Hall 悦心殿

Yuexin Hall was built in 1773, the 38th

year of Qianlong reign, on the western slope of the island. Successive emperors then met officials and dealt with political affairs there temporarily when visiting Beihai Park. There were imperial kitchens providing tea and snacks for the emperor.

Qingxiao Tower 庆霄楼

Behind Yuexin Hall, Qingxiao Tower stands erect, soaring into the sky. Since Emperor Qianlong, all emperors accompanied their mothers to the tower in the 12th month of the lunar calendar, viewing ball games being played on the ice, the major entertainment for people in winter at that time.

Yuegu Tower 阅古楼

Located at the foot of a slope on northwest Qionghua (Jade Flower) Island, Yuegu Tower was built alongside the mountain and water in 1753, the 18th year of Qianlong reign. The half - moon - shaped tower has two stories, each with five rooms. The spiral stairs were called a coiling dragon soaring to the sky. The three characters "Yuegulou" (Yuegu Tower) were handwritten by Emperor

Qianlong and inscriptions from the copybook San Xi Tang Fa Tie cover the walls inside the tower. It is the country's most complete stone carving of calligraphy, revealing the essence of Chinese calligraphy. A small room to the west of the Hall of Mental Cultivation of the Forbidden City, San Xi Tang was the private study of emperors of Qing Dynasty and where Emperor Qianlong collected handwriting samples of the great calligraphers Wang Xizhi (Kuai Xue Shi Qing Tie), Wang Xianzhi (Zhong Qiu Tie) and Wang Xun (Bo Yuan Tie). The three treasures of calligraphy gave the study its name of San Xi Tang. Emperor Qianlong ordered Liang Shizheng and other artists to inscribe on slates the 32 volumes of a collection of prestigious calligraphers since Kingdom Wei, which were then embedded into the walls of Yuegu Tower. The collection includes 340 pieces of work by134 calligraphers before the late Ming Dynasty and over 210 prefaces and postscripts, altogether 90, 000 characters. Yuegu Tower has become a paradise for calligraphy enthusiasts.

Key Words & Expressions

1. slope 斜坡
2. soar 翱翔

3. essence 精髓
4. embed 嵌入
5. prestigious 声望很高的
6. preface 前言
7. postscript 后记

Bronze Dew Plate 铜仙人承露盘

A 4.5 - meter - high white marble pillar with coiling dragons carved on its surface is on the northern side of the island, guarded by white marble balusters. A bronze immortal perches on top of the pillar and holds the lotus - shaped bronze dew plate in his hands. It is said that Emperor Wu of the Han Dynasty was devoted to Taoism, wishing to be immortal. One Taoist priest told the emperor that a mixture of dew and gems could make him so. The emperor then had the Zhang Palace built and the bronze dew plate erected in Chang'an. The plate here is the one made by Emperor Qianlong, inspired by the story of Emperor Wu, and merely served as an ornament.

Key Words & Expressions

1. baluster 栏杆
2. immortal 神仙
3. perch 站在高位

Stele of Qiong Dao Chun Yin (Qionghua Island in Shady Springtime)琼岛春阴

Located in the northeast of Qionghua (Jade Flower) Island, the stele of Qiong Dao Chun Yin (Qionghua Island in Shady Springtime) was inscribed with the handwriting of Emperor Qianlong of the Qing Dynasty during his visit here in 1761. One of the eight famous scenes of Beijing, the square stele is embellished with lotuses, enclosed by delicate stone fences. The eight famous scenes, first designated in the Jin Dynasty, were eight well-known places of interest. In the Qing Dynasty, eight steles autographed by Emperor Qianlong were erected in the eight places: Juyongguan Pass of the Great Wall, Jimen Gate outside the northwest of Deshengmen Gate, Lugou Bridge, Yuquan Mountain, Fragrant Hill, Qionghua (Jade Flower) Island of Beihai Park, the Pavilion of Zhongnanhai and the South Altar of Ritan.

Key Words & Expressions

1. stele 石碑
2. embellish 装饰
3. fragrant Hill 香山

Landscape along the Banks of Beihai Park 北海沿岸景观

West Bank 西岸

Drill Ground Stele 北海教场碑

The drill ground was built for the training of the eight-banner army in Xiyuan (inside the present-day Beihai Middle School), and a stele recording the event was erected in 1752. The drill ground stele was set up on the west bank of Beihai Park for the protection of cultural relics in 1999.

Wanfo (10,000-Buddha) Tower Stele 万佛楼石碑

Standing in front of Wanfo (10,000-Buddha) Tower, the stele was built for the 80th birthday of the mother of Emperor Qianlong. It derived its name from 10, 000 gold Buddha statues in it, plundered by the Eight-Power Allied Force in 1900, and today just the stele remains. Erected in 1770, the stele is covered with inscriptions of the Poem Celebrating the Opening of the Wanfo (10, 000-Buddha) Tower in Han, Manchu,

Mongolia and Tibet languages. It was relocated to its present location in 1987.

Key Words & Expressions

1. drill ground 教场
2. Buddha 佛
3. Manchu 满族

North Bank 北岸

Five-Dragon Pavilions 五龙亭

To the west of the north bank and to the south of the Iron Screen Wall, the Five-Dragon Pavilions were built on the original site of Taisu Hall in 1602, in the 30th year of Wanli reign of the Ming Dynasty. In 1651, Taisu Hall was pulled down and the pavilions built. This was where emperors of the Ming and Qing Dynasties fished and watched fireworks. The double-eaved one in the middle is the largest and called Longze Pavilion. Chengxiang Pavilion and Zixiang Pavilion are to its east, and Yongrui Pavilion and Fucui Pavilion to the west. Connected by zigzag bridges and white marble balusters, the five waterborne pavilions appear like a huge dragon cavorting on the lake. Hence, they were called the five-dragon pavilions. There is a single-arch stone bridge connecting each Longze

Pavilion, Zixiang Pavilion and Fucui Pavilion with the north bank. Also called Sky and Earth Pavilion, the round Longze Pavilion was for the exclusive use of the emperors, according to the saying of round sky and square earth. Concubines and officials used the square pavilions on the eastern and western sides.

Key Words & Expressions

1. Five－Dragon Pavilion 五龙亭
2. zigzag 曲折的
3. concubine 妃子

Iron Screen Wall 铁影壁

Built in the Yuan Dynasty, the Iron Screen Wall on the north bank is 1.89 meters high and its eaves are 3.56 meters long. The dark purple wall looks as if it was cast from iron, but it was actually carved from dark purple igneous rock. Legendary fierce animals and clouds are carved on the eaves, including Suanni, the ancient auspicious animal. The Iron Screen Wall, along with the Gold Block at Di'anmen Gate, the Silver Brake outside Dong'anmen Gate, the Bronze Well on north Xinjiekou Street and the Tin Hall on the north bank of Taiye Pool were listed as the five historic sites of Beijing. Of them, only the Iron Screen Wall remains in existence today.

Key Words & Expressions

1. auspicious 吉祥的
2. Gold Block 金门墩
3. Silver Brake 银闸
4. Tin Hall 锡殿

Nine-Dragon Screen 九龙壁

Built in 1756, the Nine-Dragon Screen to the north of the Iron Screen Wall is 6.65 meters high, 1.42 meters thick and 26 meters long. Standing on a jade pedestal, the screen was made of colored glazed tiles. On either side of it there are nine vivid dragons, each playing with a pearl amidst waves of clouds. Seawater, clouds and a rising sun are embedded on the eastern side; and seawater, clouds and moon on the western side. There are 635 dragons on it altogether. As a symbol of the emperor, the nine-dragon screen is superior to other ornaments. There are three nine-dragon screens in China; all are treasures of ancient architecture. The earliest, in Datong, was built in Yongle reign of the Ming Dynasty, and the most delicate is in front of Imperial Zenith Gate of the Forbidden City. The one in Beihai Park is the most special, owing to its two sides being covered with dragons.

Key Words & Expressions

1. amidst 在…当中
2. vivid 形象的
3. Imperial Zenith Gate 皇极门

Studio of Rested Heart 静心斋

Built in 1757, the Studio of Rested Heart on the north bank of Taiye Pool was originally named Jingqing Chamber. Renamed in 1913, the Studio of Rested Heart is the best - preserved and most delicate architectural feature in Beihai Park. Lovely halls in the east, tranquil temples in the west, flower walls in the south and Qionghua (Jade Flower) Island opposite it provide quiet and enchanting sights. Covering an area of 4, 800 sq meters, the studio is 110 meters long and 45 meters deep. Once Qianlong Small Garden, it was where the Emperor Qianlong played and studied. Later, it became a place for the crown prince to study and for the empress and concubines to temporarily rest on their way to worshipping Buddha. When the Eight - Power Allied Force invaded Beijing in 1900, it was the headquarters for the Japanese army. The government of the northern warlords held banquets here for their foreign masters in 1931. After the founding of the People's Republic of China, the studio was restored to its original beautiful state.

The studio consists of several courtyards of varied sizes. Jingqing Chamber greets you across the lotus pond. Standing in the water-borne Qinquan Corridor, the whole studio will come into view. On the eastern side is the delicate white marble mini jade belt bridge. On the southern side is the tranquil small courtyard with a quiet pond inside. The Zither chamber stands to the east of the corridor, the study for the crown prince of Qing Dynasty to the north, with lush bamboos dotted about. There are rockeries made of Taihu Stone to the west of the corridor. Emperor Qianlong called Zhenluan Pavilion, on the top, the palace of lotus. Diecui Tower to the northwest of the pavilion is the highest architectural item in the studio. Looking from it, you may be touched by the magnificent vista of Qionghua (Jade Flower) Island and Taiye Pool.

Key Words & Expressions

1. tranquil 宁静的

2. crown prince 皇太子
3. temporarily 暂时地
4. headquarters 总部
5. waterborne 水上的

Buddhist Temple 西天梵境

To the west of the Studio of Rested Heart we come to the Buddhist Temple, the original lamasery in Ming Dynasty, which was renovated in 1759 for the translation and printing of Buddhist Scriptures. There is a fancy glazed – tile arch outside the temple, the equivalent one in Yuanming Park was destroyed by the allied army of Britain and France in 1860. Inside the temple are two renowned steles, the left inscribed with Vajracchedika Sutra, the right one with Sutra of the Medicine Buddha. The main hall of the temple is a nanmu – structured hall, rarely seen in Beijing during the Ming Dynasty. It houses three 5 – meter – high bronze Buddha statues. In front of the main hall is the Heavenly King Hall and behind it is a two – story glazed tower. In the main hall, a huge horizontal tablet with the characters Hua Yan Qing Jie in Chinese and in the language of the Hui ethnic group is hung above. Many fancy flower decorations and small Buddha images are embedded on the glazed – tile wall outside the main hall. Accordingly, it was also called the 10,000 – Buddha Hall. The Eight – Power Allied Force plundered all the treasures here in 1900.

Key Words & Expressions

1. Buddhist Temple 西天梵境
2. Buddhist Scriptures 大藏经
3. fancy 奇特的
4. Vajracchedika Sutra 金刚经
5. Sutra of the Medicine Buddha 药师经
6. nanmu 楠木
7. Heavenly King Hall 天王殿

Silkworm Altar 先蚕坛

A green – tiled courtyard with red walls on the north bank, the Silkworm Altar was built in 1742. One of the nine altars in Beijing, the square altar is over 530 meters in circumference, surrounded by mulberries on the eastern, western and northern sides. In front of the main hall there is the altar and the stand for viewing mulberry on the southern side. Xican (washing silkworm) Pond runs to Xican (washing silkworm) River. Two wooden bridges cross the river, to the east of the southern one is the Xiling Holy Hall and to the east of the northern one the silkworm room. The Silkworm Altar was where the empresses and concubines of the Qing Dynasty annually worshipped the God of Silkworm. A restaurant and children's amusement site are now located nearby.

Key Words & Expressions

1. courtyard 大院
2. mulberry 桑树
3. worship 崇拜

East Bank 东岸

Pleasure Boat Chamber 画舫斋

On the east bank, the Pleasure Boat Chamber was also called the Water Hall. Built in 1757, it was regarded as a Xanadu of the Qing Dynasty. Prestigious artists were often invited here by the emperors of Qing Dynasty and their works displayed. Consisting of corridors around the four sides of the water, the Pleasure Boat Chamber has the characteristics of both northern courtyards and southern gardens. The waterborne chamber derived its name from its boat - shape. There is a small courtyard connected with zigzag corridors to the northwest of the chamber, where the Empress Dowager Cixi smoked opium and gambled. There stands an old sophora in the northeastern courtyard, said to have been planted in the Tang Dynasty. The old tree, the same height as the hall, is four meters in diameter. Outside the chamber is an archery range where the princes, marquis and officials competed with each other at the end of spring and the beginning of summer each year. When the Eight－Power Allied Army invaded Beijing in 1900, it became the headquarters for French invasion army. Nowadays, exhibitions of fine art and photography are frequently held here, attracting many visitors.

Key Words & Expressions

1. water hall 水殿
2. Xanadu 行宫
3. opium 鸦片
4. archery range 射箭场

Haopu Chamber 濠濮间

To the south of the Pleasure Boat Chamber, the Haopu Chamber was built according to the design brought back by the Emperor Qianlong from his tour of the south of the lower reaches of the Yangtze River in 1757. In the Qing Dynasty, the emperors usually held parties here with officials. There is a waterside pavilion in the center, surrounded by water on the eastern, western and northern sides. You can hear birds in the woods, watch fish play in the water and enjoy the green grass on the slope, an enchanting scene. There is a zigzag stone bridge across the water, at the northern end of which is a stone arch. A pair of antithetical couplets hangs on the arch, depicting the picturesque scene here. In the summer, the Empress Dowager Cixi haunted here, listening to the storytellers or gambling with concubines.

As the treasure of our garden architecture, Beihai Park has myriads of other beautiful places in addition to the above-mentioned sites. There is no doubt that its beauty, both natural and man-made, will capture you.

Key Words & Expressions

1. antithetical couplets 对联
2. picturesque 独特的
3. haunt 经常到某地
4. storyteller 说故事的人

Lifestyle of the Modern City

现代都市风情

Today's Beijing is not only renowned for its long history, but also for its rapid economic and social development. Tian'anmen Square, the Forbidden City, Jingshan Mountain and Beihai Park situated in its center symbolize a profound traditional culture, whereas modern skyscrapers represent the openness and fast tempo of the modern lifestyle. Visitors to Beijing should learn about its past and its present, so let's have a look at modern Beijing.

Xidan Culture Square
西单文化广场

Xidan Culture Square is situated to the northeast of Xidan crossing, west of Chang'an Boulevard. It occupies ground space of 21,600 sq meters and floor space of 35,000 sq meters. With flower carvings, ornaments and sculptures scattered about, people relax on seats beside the lawns and chat freely, enjoying a unique green zone in this crowded city.

The square comprises of two parts: the culture square and the underground center. The scientific gallery in the culture square features bass-relief. The two-story underground center, connected with Xidan subway station, has a shopping center, restaurants, cinemas, swimming pool, skating rink, squash field and other facilities. It is an ideal place for relaxation, entertainment and shopping.

Beijing Books Center
北京图书大厦

The Beijing Books Center to the east of Xidan Culture Square is the largest of its kind in China. Opened on May 18, 1998, the 11-story building has a floor space of over 50,000 sq meters. It has set up an on-line bookstore on Mar. 9, 1999, providing 500,000 books for 1 million visitors per year. Thus, those using on-line shopping can select their favorite books from home.

Xidan Commercial Street
西单商业街

Xidan Commercial Street is the busiest downtown area of Xidan, thronged with various stores, including Xidan Commercial Building, Xidan Shopping Center, Huawei Building, Xidan Cvik Shopping Center and

Zhongyou Department Store, etc. With the Culture Square in the east, Bank of China Building in the west facing Times Square, Xidan Commercial Street has become Beijing' s second modern commercial street, second to Wangfujing Commercial Street.

Bank of China Head Office Building
中国银行总行大厦

Standing at the northwestern corner of Xidan crossing, the Bank of China Head Office Building looks like a huge jewelry case. It cost the Bank of China a total of 2.2 billion yuan. Covering a floor space of 174, 000 sq meters, the building provides four underground parking lots. The 19 - story multi-functional building includes the banking hall, foreign exchange hall, corporate offices, conference hall, reception hall, auditorium and cafeterias, etc.

Beijing Capital Times Square
首都时代广场

Jointly built by the Construction Development Co. of Xidan Commercial Area and the Kowloon Warehouse Group, Times Square at the southeastern corner to Xidan Crossing was completed in 1999. The square is an architecture complex including offices, hotels, corporate and tenant quarters. The two－billion－yuan square occupies an area of 2.31 hectares with a floor space of over 200,000 sq meters. With two underground levels, the square consists of two areas: Area A has three－story shopping malls and 11－story office buildings; Area B has a 3－story Shopping mall. A subway will run through the square from December 2002, linking the southeastern commercial area with the northern part of Xidan. This will be greatly conducive to the prosperity and development of Xidan Commercial Street.

Qianmen Street
前门大街

Once a prestigious commercial street in the Yuan, Ming and Qing Dynasties, Qianmen Street now ranks in one of the three traditional commercial streets of Beijing, coupled with Wangfujing Commercial Street and North Xidan Commercial Street. First built in the Yuan Dynasty, it was frequented by nobles, high - ranking officials and tourists visiting Beijing during the Ming and Qing Dynasties. It was also the closest commercial street to the Forbidden City. The 2 - km street stretches from Qianmen Gate in the north to Yongdingmen Gate in the south. The area neighboring Dazhalan in the north used to be the most bustling area, carrying much traditional characteristics of old Beijing city. Many stores with long - standing bistory remain today, including the Ruifuxiang Silk and Satin Store, which has been here since 1893, Tongrentang Pharmacy since 1669, Liubiju Pickle Store since 1530, Quanjude Roast Duck

Restaurant and Douyichu Steamed Dumpling. Qianmen Street provides a world of the old Beijing lifestyle.

Wangfujing Commercial Street 王府井大街

The most renowned commercial street, it has been regarded as the golden street. A number of official establishments and residences of the princes existed here 700 years ago. In the Ming and Qing Dynasties, it developed into a prosperous commercial street. A well of sweet water on the street led to its name---Wangfujing (well of the residence of the prince). Since the old narrow street obstructed the city's development, the Beijing Municipality renovated it. Today's 1.6-km-long street includes the Oriental Plaza, Beijing Hotel, China National Arts & Crafts Building, Haoyou World, New Dong' an Market, Tianlun Dynasty Hotel and the Capital Theatre, etc. There are green lawns, flowerbeds, fountains and seating for relaxation. Its famous snack food street, with its abundant food, may suffice you with special delights.

Beijing Hotel
北京饭店

Beijing Hotel, to the west of the south exit of Wangfujing Commercial Street, is the oldest and most special hotel of long-standing history. The three parts of the hotel clearly represent different ages. The light cream-colored middle section has seven stories and over 140 rooms. Built by the French in 1917, the 40-meter-high section embodies a typical European style. It is the earliest and highest-class hotel in Beijing. The deep brown mid-west section has eight stories and more than 240 rooms. This 44-meter-high section with its unique traditional Chinese style was built in 1954. In its large and palatial banquet hall, the late Prime Minister Zhou Enlai once held a grand reception. The orange eastern section consists of 23 stories and over 600 rooms. This 89-meter-high modern skyscraper was built in 1974.

Grand Hotel
贵宾楼饭店

The 10 - story orange - colored building to the west of Beijing Hotel is 41 meters high, with 287 presidential suites and stately hotel rooms. The Beijing Hotel Group and Hong Kong celebrity Mr. Huo Yingdong cosponsored it in 1989. This modern hotel integrates both traditional Chinese and Western architecture styles.

Oriental Plaza
东方广场

Construction of the Oriental Plaza, to the east of the south exit of Wangfujing Commercial Street, began in 1997 and was completed in 2000. It has a ground space of 110, 000 sq meters and floor space of 900, 000 sq meters, and cost US $1.94 billion. Cosponsored by the Beijing Honglian Culture Co. Ltd and the

Hong Kong Huixian Investment Co. of Mr. Li Ka Shing and Mr. C.C. Tung, the plaza features a shopping center, office buildings, apartments and five-star hotel, etc. There is a Palaeoanthropology Ruins Museum underground, featuring items discovered during construction. The plaza has a uniquely favorable geographical advantage, with Wangfujing Commercial Street in the west, North Dongdan Street in the east and Chang'an Boulevard in the south. Coupled with Wangfujing Commercial Street and North Dongdan Street, it has become the most renowned international commercial center and the largest commercial complex in Asia.

North Dongdan Street
东单北大街

The name of the street originates from the Ming and Qing Dynasties, when it had odd-numbered arches to the east of Chang'an Boulevard. The present 1.6-km-long street abounds in franchised stores selling foreign brand clothing, including Apple, Crocodile,

Gold Lion and Robinhood, etc. There are many relevant facilities, including shopping centers, restaurants and entertainment places.

Key Words & Expressions

1. renowned for 以…闻名
2. profound 深厚的
3. skyscraper 摩天大楼
4. Xidan Culture Square 西单文化广场
5. ground space 占地面积
6. floor space 建筑面积
7. scientific gallery 科普画廊
8. skating rink 溜冰场
9. squash field 壁球场
10. Beijing Book Luilding 北京图书大厦
11. Commercial Street 商业街
12. Zhongyou Department Store 中友百货
13. second to… 仅次于
14. jewelry case 首饰盒
15. corporate office 写字楼
16. hectare 公顷
17. conducive to 有助于…
18. frequent 经常光临
19. stores of long-standing history 老字号
20. pharmacy 药店
21. steamed dumpling 烧麦
22. Roast Duck 烤鸭

23. obstruct 阻碍

24. China National Arts & Crafts Building 工美大厦

25. Oriental Plaza 东方广场

26. Capital Theatre 首都剧场

27. suffice 满足

28. palatial 富丽堂皇的

29. integrate 结合

30. commercial complex 商务建筑群体

Tour Instructions 游览须知

Tian'anmen Gate Tower 天安门城楼

Tel: 63095745

Open: 8:00 - 17:00 (last entry at 16:30)

Admission Fees: adult: 15 yuan per person; student: 5 yuan per person

Memorial Hall of Chairman Mao 毛主席纪念堂

Tel: 65132277

Open: 8:30 - 11:30am (Tuesday - Sunday)

14:00 - 16:00pm (Tuesday - Thursday)

Admission Fee: free

Zhengyangmen Gate Tower 正阳门城楼

Tel: 63017994

Open: 8:30 - 16:00

Admission Fee: Adult: 5 yuan per person; Student: 3 yuan per person

Great Hall of the People 人民大会堂

Tel: 63096156

Open: flexible. Same as other halls, It is

closed at noon. Pre – telephone inquiry is preferred.

Admission Fee: Adult: 20 yuan per person; Student: 10 yuan per person

Museum of Chinese History 中国历史博物馆

Tel: 65128321

Open: 8:30 – 16:30 (last entry at 15:30)

Admission Fee: Pre – telephone inquiry is preferred, as the exhibition contents are often changed.

Museum of Chinese Revolution 中国革命博物馆

Tel: 65128967

Open: 8:30 – 16:30

Admission Fee: Pre – telephone inquiry is preferred, as the exhibition contents are often changed.

Zhongshan Park 中山公园

Tel: 66055431

Open: 6:00 – 21:00

Admission Fee: Adult: 3 yuan per person; Student: 1.5 yuan per person

Working People's Cultural Palace 劳动人民文化宫

Tel: 65253113

Open: 6:00-21:00

Admission Fee: Adult: 2 yuan per person; Student: 1 yuan. 15 yuan per person to visit the Chinese Serial Bells; 5 yuan to visit the exhibition of worshipping ancestors

Jingshan Park 景山公园

Tel: 64044071

Open: 6:00-21:00

Admission Fee: Adult: 10 yuan per person; Student: 5 yuan per person

Beihai Park 北海公园

Tel: 64040610

Open: 6:00-21:00

Admission Fee: Adult: 10 yuan per person; Student: 5 yuan per person. Tour of Qionghua (Jade Flower) Island: 10 yuan per person

Annals of the emperors of the Ming Dynasty
明朝皇帝纪年表
(1368～1644)

Name	Title of an emperor's reign	Posthumous Title of Honor	Age when enthroned	Reign Period
Zhu Yuanzhang	Hong Wu	Taizu	41	1368～1398
Zhu Yunwen	Jian Wen		22	1398～1402
Zhu Di	Yong Le	Chengzu	43	1402～1424
Zhu Gaochi	Hong Xi	Renzong	47	1424～1425
Zhu Zhanji	Xuan De	Xuanzong	28	1425～1435
Zhu Qizhen	Zheng Tong	Yingzong	9	1435～1449
Zhu Qiyu	Jing Tai	Daizong	22	1449～1457
Zhu Qizhen	Tian Shun	Yingzong	31	1457～1464
Zhu Jianshen	Cheng Hua	Xianzong	18	1464～1487
Zhu Youtang	Hong Zhi	Xiaozong	18	1487～1505
Zhu Houzhao	Zheng De	Wuzong	15	1505～1521
Zhu Houcong	Jia Jing	Shizong	15	1521～1566
Zhu Zaihou	Long Qing	Muzong	30	1566～1572
Zhu Yijun	Wan Li	Shenzong	10	1572～1620
Zhu Changluo	Tai Chang	Guangzong	39	Aug. －Sept., 1620
Zhu Youxiao	Tian Qi	Xizong	16	1620～1627
Zhu Youjian	Chong Zhen	Sizong	18	1627～1644

Annals of the emperors of the Qing Dynasty

清朝皇帝纪年表

(1644～1912)

Name	Title of an emperor's reign	Posthumous Title of Honor	Age when enthroned	Reign Period
Fu Lin	Shun Zhi	Shizu	6	1644～1661
Xuan Ye	Kang Xi	Shengzu	8	1662～1722
Yin zhen	Yong Zheng	Shizong	45	1722～1735
Hong Li	Qian Long	Gaozong	25	1735～1795
Yong Yan	Jia Qing	Renzong	37	1795～1820
Ming Ning	Dao Guang	Xuanzong	39	1820～1850
Yi Ning	Xian Feng	Wenzong	20	1850～1861
Zai Chun	Tong Zhi	Muzong	6	1861～1874
Zai Tian	Guang Xu	Dezong	4	1874～1908
Pu Yi	Xuan Tong		3	1908～1912

中文

天安门

天安门，坐落在北京市中心南北中轴线上，横跨东西的长安街从天安门前横穿而过，使天安门与广场上的其他建筑既彼此联系，又相对独立。从过去明清两代皇城的正门到今天北京和中国的象征，天安门已经历了数百年的人事沧桑和历史变迁。每一位来北京观光的中外游客，都不禁会为天安门的雄伟、开阔所震撼，为整个天安门广场厚重的历史文化所感染。

作为北京著名的旅游景点，天安门、天安门广场以及广场上的每一座建筑，都成了传递中华文化的使者，在一年胜似一年的旅游热潮中，为更多的中外游人所了解。为了更好地了解天安门的过去和现在，我们首先从天安门广场谈起。

一、天安门广场

1. 世界名城中最大的广场

天安门广场，就像莫斯科的红场、巴黎的凯旋门、华盛顿的纪念碑一样，是中国首都北京的标志性建筑物。在1992年“北京旅游世界之最”的评定中，天安门广场当选为“世界上最大的城市中心广场”。它以其悠久的历史和雄伟的身姿，每年吸引着数以百万计的游客观光游览，成为向国内外游客展示北京风采的第一“形象大使”。

天安门广场，位于北京市中心的中轴线上，北起天安门红墙，南至正阳门城楼（前门），西至人民大会堂，东至中国革命博物馆和中国历史博物馆，南北长880米，东西宽500米，占地面积达44万多平方米，可同时容纳约100万人举行各种盛大的集会。开国大典和历次国庆阅兵式都是在这里举行，场面恢宏庞大，壮丽无比。就是在这样的盛大场面下，天安门广场见证着共和国成长中迈出的每一个坚定的步伐。

2. 天安门广场的历史演变

早在辽、金时期，北京就已成为北部中国的政治中心。其著名的佛教寺院——兴国寺就建在当今的中山公园附近。蒙古族铁骑入主中原，将北京作为其首都，开始营建元大都。元大都外城的正南门——丽正门，就在今天的天安门南。也就是说，今天的天安门广场，早在元大都时，就已是进出皇城的必经之地。但真正奠定现在天安门广场格局的还是明代永乐皇帝迁都北京之后。

明永乐十五年(1417年),皇城的正门——承天门建成,即今天的天安门。另外,在皇城的最南端还建有大明门(清朝改为大清门,民国时为中华门),即今天毛主席纪念堂的位置。大明门左右两侧伸出两道红墙,分别向东向西,再折而向北,并在今东长安街西口、西长安街东口,建有长安左门和长安右门。城墙继续往北,与承天门城墙相接,形成一个"T"形广场,是天安门城楼前举行皇家活动的重要场所,这便是今天天安门广场的最早雏形。

民国初年,政府打破皇城附近禁止随意穿行的规定,首先开辟了天安门的东西大道,神武门与景山之间也允许市民通过,从而打通了紫禁城南北和东西两条交通干线。后来,又拆除一些防碍交通的城墙和侧门,基本形成一个小广场。

新中国成立后,对天安门广场进行了多次扩建,从而形成了现在天安门广场可容纳100万人的规模。

3. 天安门广场上的棋盘街与千步廊

明清时的棋盘街,指的是今天天安门广场最南端,毛主席纪念堂南门至正阳门城楼下这片空地。明代以木栏围着,中间有一条东西向的通道,好像棋盘的"楚河"、"汉界"。清代乾隆皇帝时,对棋盘街进行修葺,将原来象棋盘的两座木栅,改成了一座正方形的石栅栏,象棋盘变了形,倒有点像围棋盘了。棋盘街在明清时是商贾荟萃、市井繁华的贸易、娱乐之所。对于普通百姓来说，能在天子禁城脚下叫卖各种风味小吃、表演戏曲、杂技等，简直是一种莫大的荣幸，故而棋盘街又有“天街”之称。

千步廊，是指大清门（今毛主席纪念堂位置）以里沿“T”形广场东南西三面建造的白玉阶基的通脊连檐的长廊，共有朝房144间。长安左门和东千步廊是举行“金榜题名”的场所。考生参加完皇帝亲自主持的殿试后两天，要在殿上传呼考中进士的考生的姓名，称“金殿传胪”。金殿传胪后，把黄榜放入龙亭，进士随礼部官员出御道到长安左门外，将黄榜张挂在临时搭建的“龙棚”里。考生榜上有名者，大都喜笑颜开，犹如鲤鱼跃龙门，所以人们又称长安左门为“龙门”。而长安右门和西千步廊，在明清之际则是进行“秋审”和“朝审”的场所。犯人先由长安右门进广场受审，被朱笔勾决者一般在冬至那天的清早，被押送到宣武门外的菜市口行刑。犯人一脚踏进长安右门，便犹如身陷虎口，难以活命，故长安右门又被称为“虎门”。一边是金榜题名，一边将肝脑涂地，普通百姓的荣辱往往系于君主的一念之间！

4. 昔日广场上的白丁香与黄刺玫

当我们今天漫步在广阔的天安门广场时，除了碧绿的人工草皮以及节日装饰性花雕外，谁会想到就在几十年前，这里还种植着很多白丁香与黄刺玫呢？

辛亥革命以后，新建的民国政府并没有几日的安宁,就陷入了军阀混战当中。本已满目疮痍的北京又遭受了日军的八年践踏。在这样内忧外患的年代，天安门广场一直是广大人民群众进行爱国运动的重要阵地。封建军阀和国民党统治者为了镇压学生和人民的爱国运动，在天安门前种植了许多白丁香和黄刺玫，以缩小广场的面积,阻止群众的示威游行活动。这样，本来美丽圣洁的花朵却成了阴谋与邪恶的代名词。

5. 天安门广场的扩建与开放

新中国成立后，天安门广场进行了三次主要的扩建。第一次是在 1949 年，也就是新中国国成立的第一年，主要是对原广场的整理、修缮与美化工作。开国大典就是在第一次修缮、扩建完成之后举行的。第二次是在 1958 年，为了迎接建国十周年大庆，天安门广场进行了一次规模最大的扩建，从而奠定了南北长 880 米，东西宽 500 米的格局。人民大会堂、人民英雄纪念碑、中国历史博物馆和中国革命博物馆都是在这次扩建中应运而生的。第三次扩建是在 1976 年，一代伟人毛泽东去世后，人们在人民英雄纪念碑和正阳门之间建造了毛主席纪念堂，以表达对这位伟人永远的哀思。三次扩建后的天安门广场，已经形成了今天天安门广场上的整个建筑布局。它稳健地坐落于北京的中心，向人们展示着中华文化的独特韵味。

6. 天安门广场上的升降旗仪式

1991年5月1日起，人们在天安门广场开始执行市政府颁布的升（降）国旗仪式的规定，在每月1日、11日、21日或逢国家重要庆典（如元旦、春节、五一国际劳动节、七一党的生日、八一建军节、十一国庆节等）时，举行节日升（降）旗仪式，军乐队现场演奏《义勇军进行曲》；其他日子举行平日升（降）旗仪式，播放国歌录音。从那时起，天安门广场上的升（降）旗仪式，就成了中外广大游客到北京旅游时喜爱观瞻的一大胜景。

升旗用的旗杆是用首钢生产的无缝钢管制成的，分四节，重7吨，高32. 6米。经过特殊处理，保证20年不会锈蚀。

每天，当太阳从地平线上升起的时候，鲜艳的五星红旗也会在雄壮嘹亮的国歌声的伴奏下，在天安门广场冉冉升起，象征着伟大祖国如旭日东升、前程无限；降旗时间，以日落时间为准。五星红旗在演奏国歌的第一个音符启动至最后一个音符结束，准时升到38米高的旗杆顶端，整个过程2分07秒。升（降）旗仪式已经成为天安门广场的重要景观。为了方便游人观瞻，广场中设有次日的升（降）国旗时间的预报。每天，由96人（以表示捍卫祖国960万平方公里的神圣领土）组成的国旗护卫队的队员们，穿着笔挺的制服，肩扛半自动步枪，在1名肩扛五星红旗的擎旗手、2名护旗手的带领下，在雄壮的军乐声中，迈着整齐坚定的步伐，走出天安门。从金水桥至旗杆围栏，准正步138步，落地同声，动作一致。队员们走如风、站如松、横成列、纵成行，充分显示了中华民族的顽强精神和伟大祖国的光辉形象。

二、天安门城楼

1. 天安门城楼的建筑特色及主要作用

我们现在常说的天安门，主要是指天安门城楼而言。天安门，原是明清两代皇城的正门，始建于明永乐十五年（1417年），建成于明永乐十八年(1420年)。天安门原名承天门，即“承天启运”，“受命于天”之意，被视为皇朝承天命和敬天地的重要场所。它初建时只是六柱五门的木牌坊，后被火烧毁重建，成为一座面阔九间、进深五间的门楼，以体现帝王的“九五之尊”。明末，承天门再次毁于兵火，清顺治八年(1651年)重修时，改名为天安门。当时，顺治帝将故宫前朝三大殿分别改名为太和殿、中和殿、保和殿，殿名均带“和”字；将皇城四门分别改名为天安门、地安门、东安门和西安门，门名均带“安”字，寄托了皇帝希望国家“内和外安”的美好愿望。

天安门由城基、城台、城楼三部分组成，总高度为34.7米。城基高1.59米，城台高14.6米，由每块420公斤重的石头砌成。城楼上，东西两端各建有3间黄瓦红墙、红窗的小房子，它们是守护天安门城楼护军的住房，其守军担负着眺望和守护城楼的任务。

明清两代，皇帝每逢冬至祭天、夏至祭地、孟春祈谷、仲夏亲耕，以及皇帝大婚、出兵等隆重典礼，皇帝及随从人员都从天安门出入。另外，皇帝登基、册立皇后、册立太子等大事，都在天安门城楼上举行颁诏仪式。

新中国成立后，一些重大仪式如开国大典，共和国生日大庆典等，党和国家领导人也会登上天安门城楼，与人民群众一起庆祝祝福。

2. 天安门城楼与“金凤颁诏”

明清两代帝王颁发诏书，是要举行一定仪式的，这种仪式有一个很好听的名字，即“金凤颁诏”。明代颁诏时，用一根龙头杆系彩绳顺墙而下。清代颁诏时，在天安门正中设宣诏台，宣诏后，众官员行三跪九叩礼，宣诏官将诏书放在一个镀金雕云状的“朵云”盘内，然后来到城楼正中，将诏书用黄丝线悬系在一木雕金凤的口中，金凤口衔诏书徐徐而下，好像天子帝王之命由金凤乘云朵自天空而降落到人间。礼部官员仍用云朵盘接承诏书，放入龙亭后送到礼部，由礼部将诏书印好，颁行天下。这一整个过程被称为“金凤颁诏”。

历史上在天安门城楼举行的最后一次“金凤颁诏”仪式，是1912年2月12日颁布末代皇帝溥仪的退位诏书仪式。1911年，辛亥革命推翻了清王朝的统治，但直到1912年，隆裕皇太后才以宣统皇帝的名义颁布退位诏书，决定接受共和政体。这份诏书用墨笔在普通纸上书写而成，长53厘米，宽21.5厘米，仍按照以前金凤颁诏的程序进行颁布。但此时的清王室，只是在新政府的优待政策下，才得以继续住在昔日的皇宫里，维持那仅有的一点尊严，哪里还有心情再讲从前“金凤颁诏”的排场。历史上的最后一次“金凤颁诏”就是这样灰溜溜地退出了中国历史的舞台。

3.“大红灯笼高高挂”

现在我们走在节日的天安门广场上时，只要一抬头，就可以看到悬挂在天安门城楼上的新式宫灯。但我相信，很多人可能都从有关开国大典的电视记录片或图片上看到过挂在天安门城楼上的八盏大红灯笼。它们在开国大典上正式投入使用，记载着共和国成长的历史进程。您也许会问：“它们哪去了”？

其实，那八盏大红灯笼在1994年国庆前夕才为新式宫灯所取代。其中三对由天安门管委会和有关博物馆收藏，东二和西二位置上的两只灯笼以1380万元的价格被拍卖，拍卖所得捐献给北京贫困山区解决饮水问题和“希望工程”。这八盏大灯笼，也算是有史以来最大的宫灯了，每一盏都有2.23米高，周长8.05米，直径2.25米，重达80公斤。更让我们想不到的是，这八盏大红灯笼的设计者竟然是两位日本人。由此可见,中日两国人民一直进行着友好的文化交流。

4. 城楼上的毛主席肖像

天安门城楼正中门上，悬挂着一幅中国人民最敬仰的毛泽东主席的画像。画像两侧是两幅巨型标语:西侧是“中华人民共和国万岁”,东侧是“世界人民大团结万岁”。这幅画像，高6米,宽4.6米,加上像框,总重量达1.5吨,堪称全国最大的手工绘制肖像了。画像长年挂在外面，自然免不了风吹雨淋，为了保证画像的效果,一般每年要更换一次。新的画像总是在十一国庆节前挂到天安门上。

5. 天安门城楼与开国大典

新中国的成立，是中国历史上一件举足轻重的大事。随着毛泽东主席在天安门城楼上庄严地宣告:“中华人民共和国成立了”,中国人民便开始了历史的新篇章。就在开国大典仪式上,毛泽东主席亲自将五星红旗升上天安门广场的上空。广场上30万人民群众一齐肃立致敬,尽情享受着属于那一时刻的幸福与快乐。相信很多经历了那一时刻的人，至今对那种宏大场面仍记忆犹新。

6. 天安门城楼上的三发炮弹

天安门城楼作为首都北京核心的标志性建筑,既记载着建国时的喜悦,也同时记载着中华民族的屈辱。

1952年,在对天安门进行重修的过程中,工人们在城楼西边的木梁上发现了三颗未爆炸的炮弹，弹壳上还有几个隐约可见的英文字母。这自然让我们想起八国联军炮击天安门城楼的惨烈一幕。

1900年，长期遭受封建主义和帝国主义双重压迫的中国人民在北京发动了义和团运动。帝国主义早已看穿了清政府的懦弱无能，由英、法、德、美、日、意、奥、俄组成了2000多人的八国联军，进犯北京。他们烧毁了正阳门箭楼之后，又集中射击天安门，就连天安门旁边太庙正殿屋脊上的螭吻也被击毁。这三发炮弹便是当时联军入侵并毁坏文物的罪证。

7. 天安门城楼的开放

天安门城楼在明清两代是皇城的正门，它直通皇帝居住的紫禁城，普通百姓只能远远地观望，登上城楼在那时看来，真的就比登天还难。新中国成立后，百姓虽然可以穿过天安门，到皇家禁地去看一看，但仍然没有机会登上天安门城楼，一睹北京首都最大的城市中心广场。直到1988年1月1日，天安门城楼才正式向中国和世界人民开放。第一位登上天安门城楼的是北京的一位75岁的老人，而最早登上城楼的外国游客则是一对来自法国的夫妇，他们都收到了一只景泰蓝花瓶和证书，以纪念这个不平凡的日子。

三、外金水河与外金水桥

1. 金水河名称的由来及主要作用

天安门前蜿蜒流过的河流被称为金水河。按照阴阳五行之说，"金"对应着"西"，而河中的水由西向东流过，故名金水河。因紫禁城内也有一条金水河，为了区分，一般将这条河称为外金水河，而紫禁城内的则称为内金水河。金水河除了可以美化环境，使枯燥的红墙黄瓦为主体的建筑中涌入一股清新之外，它还为宫廷内的消防提供水源，并在夏天的暴雨之时起到泄水的作用。

2. 荷花、蟠龙见等级

碧波涟涟的外金水河上，南北纵跨七座洁白美丽的石桥，中间五座统称为外金水桥，与天安门的五个门洞相对应。每座桥身都是中间窄高，两端宽低，充分展示了弧线的装饰美化效果。如果仔细观察，我们会发现桥上两侧汉白玉石栏杆柱头上雕刻的图案有些不同，中间桥上雕刻的是条条蟠龙，而其他桥上雕刻的则是朵朵莲花。为什么会在桥的柱头图案上存在这样的差别呢？其实，这与桥的功用、等级是联系在一起的。

五座桥当中，正中间的桥最宽，被称为"御路桥"，明清两代是只有皇帝才可以从上面出入的，因而以蟠龙作为柱头的装饰，代表皇权的至高无上。其他以莲花为装饰的四座桥,用途也是不一样的。御路桥两旁的称为“王公桥”,为宗室王公出入皇宫时所专用;再外侧两桥为“品级桥”,供三品以上文武官员通行使用。除这五座桥外,距离稍远的两侧,即今天的中山公园和劳动人民文化宫前,也有两座桥,被称为“公生桥”,分别是供四品以下的官吏、兵士、工役、宫女、太监受召出入宫廷时使用。这些桥的使用有着严格的等级界限,不得有丝毫的违规逾越。

清代皇帝从天安门出行举行祭祀仪式时,“扈从仪仗”要先分五路出天安门,然后按等级分成七路通过相应的石桥。但按等级经过金水桥的规定,只是随皇帝出入时方起作用,平时上下朝,不管是几品官吏,一律走东西的公生桥。

3. **石狮**

(1)狮子与龙子

金水桥前,左右两侧各蹲有一座威武庄严的汉白玉石狮子。在中国古代因为狮子威武凶猛,有百兽之王之封。后来,人们将狮子与龙附会到一起,在民间传说中狮子被认为是龙的第八子,被称为“狻猊”。因其喜欢烟火,经常被装饰在香炉盖上。慢慢地,狮子就成了至高无上的皇权的化身了,多被摆放在皇宫大院的门前,用以避邪驱灾,代表庄严与神圣。

(2)雄狮与雌狮

雄踞在天安门前的一对石狮,一左一右,一雄一雌。左边的为雄狮,脚踏一只大绣球,象征着皇帝拥有广大的国土和至高无上的权力；右边为雌狮,左脚下是一只可爱的小狮子,象征皇后母仪天下。如果不注意两只狮子脚下的细小差别,我们是很难辨别这两只狮子的雌雄的。单从狮子的相貌来看,两只都像雄狮。据说,这主要是因为中国古代人们所见到的狮子，多是外国使节进贡的雄狮，所以石匠们在创作狮子的时候，就自然想到以绣球和小狮子来区分雌雄。不论这种说法是真是假,天安门前的这对石狮都始终把守在金水河前，昂首注视着多年来广场上发生的每一点细微变化。或许,它们也正在为北京的巨变而骄傲呢。

4. 华表与“诽谤木”

天安门的内外，各有一对高近 10 米的汉白玉精雕石柱,这便是我们熟悉的“华表”。华表在中国有着久远的历史。相传,在原始社会的尧舜禹时代就已有此物，那时的华表是用来标示道路的木桩,就像现在的指路标。据史籍记载,舜时，他允许普通百姓在木桩上刻写对统治者的建议，以体察民情，弥补时政得失，这种木桩被称为“诽谤木”。随着时代的演变,君主已不再需要用这种方式来体察民情了，于是原来的木桩子逐渐变成了今天的汉白玉石雕，雕刻上象征皇权的云龙图案,放置于皇宫或陵寝的门前,作为皇家建筑的一种标志。

5. 华表上的“望天犼”

华表上面，是一圆盘，称为承露盘，承露盘

上蹲立一怪兽“望天犼”。盘下，横插有两块云板。中间的石柱上，缠绕一四足五爪的游龙，翻腾于祥云之间。华表下面是一八角形的须弥基座，底部是一方形石栏，四角有柱，每一柱上蹲有一只小石狮。华表与须弥座一起，高达 9.57 米。关于华表上方的怪兽“望天犼”，还流传着这样的说法：望天犼高高蹲立在华表上，时刻注视着帝王的一切行动。当帝王外出巡幸或私访久久不归时，望天犼会告诫皇帝赶紧归来，处理朝内事务。这指的是天安门外的两只头向南方的望天犼，称为“望君归”。相应的，天安门内的两只望天犼则被称为“望君出”，头向北方紫禁城的方向，注视着后宫，即当皇帝久居后宫与后妃们消遣娱乐的时候，劝诫皇帝不要只顾沉溺于宫中的生活，应该出来到民间走一走，以体察民间的疾苦。

6. 华表“搬家”

我们今天在天安门前看到的华表，和原来的相比已被往后移动了 6 米。您可能要问：这么大的华表，为什么要移动，又是怎么移动的呢？

要弄清这个问题，还得从八国联军侵华的屈辱史谈起。1900 年 8 月 13 日夜，八国联军攻到北京城下，他们在野蛮地炮轰前门箭楼和城楼之后，便疯狂地炮击天安门城楼，以致城墙倒塌，西侧的华表也被炸掉一块。新中国成立后，因天安门广场要扩建，这对重达 2 万多公斤的华表经修复后需要向后移动 6 米，但又决不能让华表受到丝毫损坏。这是一项很艰巨的任务，可能我们都不会想到，如此一项艰巨的任务却是由一位64岁的老人来完成的。

这位老人名叫徐荣，祖上几代一直负责为宫廷建筑搭架子，并且负责殡葬皇帝的“金棺”。他就是利用类似于以前吊运“金棺”的方法，用一些木桩、麻绳、吊链，将偌大的华表吊起后向后移动了6米，放到现在的位置上去的。由此可见，在每一杰作的后面，都蕴藏着劳动人民的无穷智慧。

四、人民英雄纪念碑

1. 碑体及碑文介绍

人民英雄纪念碑位于天安门广场五星红旗基座之南，是为纪念1840～1949年间为革命牺牲的人民英雄而建立的。这座高大塔碑由梁思成等人设计，于1952年8月1日动土修建，1958年4月竣工。全碑用花岗岩和汉白玉石块共1.7万块，通高37.94米，碑座占地约3000平方米。主体碑石由一整块花岗岩制成，长14.7米，宽2.9米，厚1米，重达103吨。整座纪念碑巍然屹立于天安门广场中央，距天安门墙基440米，在天安门广场的正中央，显得非常庄严稳重。

人民英雄纪念碑的正面面向天安门，碑心石上雕刻着毛主席亲笔题写的八个镏金大字：

“人民英雄永垂不朽”。碑身正面，是毛主席著文,周总理亲笔书写的碑文：

三年以来，在人民解放战争和人民革命中牺牲的人民英雄们永垂不朽!

三十年以来，在人民解放战争和人民革命中牺牲的人民英雄们永垂不朽!

由此上溯到一千八百四十年,从那时起,为了反对内外敌人，争取民族独立和人民自由幸福，在历次斗争中牺牲的人民英雄们永垂不朽!

2. 碑顶和浮雕图案

纪念碑的碑顶,采用的是上有卷云,下有重幔的传统建筑形式的小庑殿顶。既体现民族传统风格,又突出碑身的主体设计。纪念碑的主题浮雕图案,最早由著名历史学家范文澜拟定,经毛主席批示和党中央多次讨论后确定为现在的八幅浮雕，即从碑身东面起，按其历史顺序排列,依次为:鸦片战争、金田起义、武昌起义、五四运动、五卅运动、南昌起义、抗日游击战争、胜利渡江。浮雕高 2 米,全长 40.68 米,由八位雕塑专家及其助手共同完成。

碑身东西两侧的上部,刻着以红星、松柏和旗帜组成的“光辉永照”的装饰花纹，象征着革命精神万年长存。小碑座的周围,刻以牡丹、荷花、菊花等组成的 8 个大花圈，象征着“高贵”、“纯洁”、“坚忍”,表示全国人民对英雄们的永远怀念和敬仰。

3.“人民英雄永垂不朽”镏金文字

人民英雄纪念碑正面的八个镏金大字“人民英雄永垂不朽”是我们再熟悉不过的了。这八个字原由毛主席写到信纸上，经投影机放大20倍后按照光影描绘而成。放大后的字，仅仅一个“永”字就有2米多高。这八个大字，是采用我国传统的镏金工艺，做成金字镶嵌进去的，可以保证较长时间不变色。据载，纪念碑上的八字碑题和碑文共用黄金130两，体现了我国镏金工艺的高超水平。

五、毛主席纪念堂

1. 简介

1976年9月9日，伟大领袖毛泽东主席与世长辞。为了保存毛主席的遗体，以便人民纪念和瞻仰，中央作出了修建毛主席纪念堂的决定。堂址选在天安门广场人民英雄纪念碑与正阳门之间，面北背南，与天安门相对。1976年11月24日，纪念堂正式奠基，并于次年5月竣工。这是一座方形建筑，占地面积2.8万平方米，四周为44根八角形的花岗岩石柱。南北庭院中间，是两组8.7米高的巨大雕塑。整座建筑气势恢宏，衬托了毛主席一生的光辉伟大。

2. 中央瞻仰厅

毛主席纪念堂的北厅，是中央瞻仰厅，迎面正中央为汉白玉石雕毛主席坐像，高达3.45

米。这一雕像,共花费石料40多立方米,历时半年多才雕刻完成。主席面容慈祥,体态魁梧,显得十分和蔼亲切。

毛主席坐像背后,衬托着一幅“大好河山”的绒绣壁毯。这幅绒绣壁毯,以祖国大好河山为主画面,以衬托主席高瞻远瞩的伟大革命气魄。而这幅绒绣壁毯的制作,也是非同一般的。画稿设计完成以后,43位出色的女绣工用了58个日日夜夜,640多万针,将近300公斤绒线才织完这幅高7米,长24米,令人赞羡不已的绒绣。其所用颜色就多达1200多种,而且首先采用了金线和彩色绒线,显示了中国高超的刺绣水平。

瞻仰厅是纪念堂的核心部分。厅的正中央砌有一座黑色花岗岩石棺座,上面停放着载有毛主席遗体的水晶棺,四周鲜花环绕。遗体为中国共产党党旗覆盖,显得安详而肃穆。水晶棺的制作和安放,都有着极高的技术要求,既要防水防尘,又要防震,而且要满足在瞻仰时,遗体上升到水晶棺中,而夜晚则需降至地下,以便于遗体的保存。遗体周围的各种绢花、松枝,也是防水防尘的,它能保持较长时间不变色,就像毛主席在人民心目中的地位一样,是永远不会改变的。

3.纪念堂的开放及其他领袖人物的纪念室

1977年9月9日,毛泽东主席逝世一周年时,纪念堂正式开放。但那时是凭票参观的,

1984 年 7 月 1 日，正式取消了票证，游人们可以排队按秩序瞻仰毛主席遗容。第一位走进纪念堂的外国元首，是南斯拉夫的总书记铁托。现在，每天有数以万计的观众来瞻仰主席遗容，这里已成为向全国人民进行革命教育的基地。

后来，随着老一辈革命领导人的相继去逝，1988 年，在纪念堂东西两侧分别设立了毛泽东、刘少奇、周恩来、朱德同志的革命业绩纪念室，内有大批文物、图片、书信、文献等资料，供游人参观学习。近年，这里又新增了邓小平和陈云同志的纪念室。

六、前门(正阳门)

1. 北京的城门

明清时的北京城，共分成四层，分别为外城、内城、皇城和宫城。每一层都由厚厚的城墙围护，并开有相应的城门。像我们熟悉的天安门就是以前皇城的正门，宫城的正门则是紫禁城的午门。正阳门即今天我们看到的前门，是原北京内城的正门。原来的内城城墙，大致相当于今天二环路的范围。当您坐上地铁环线的时候，还可以听到前门、崇文门、宣武门、阜成门、西直门、德胜门、安定门、东直门、朝阳门这些名字，这就是原来内城的九个城门。新中国成立后，由于城市规划的需要，老北京城的城墙、城门几乎都被拆掉了，内城城门现在只有正阳门和德胜门保存下来留作纪念。

明清两代,内城城门的使用,也有严格的规定。正阳门是正门,为皇室车辆出入时专用,崇文门走酒车,宣武门走囚车,阜成门走煤车,西直门走水车,德胜门走兵车,安定门走粪车,东直门走木材车,朝阳门走粮车,各门行走规定分工明确,秩序井然。

2. 正阳门及其作用

内城九门当中,目前知名度最高的要算是正阳门了,即今天的前门。因古代以南为阳,以南为正,"日者众阳之宗",故称正阳门。又因为它位于紫禁城与皇城的正前方,所以俗称前门。

正阳门,建于明永乐十八年(1420年),城楼高42米。正阳门为双重城门楼,北侧为主门,即正阳门城楼,南侧为箭楼,上面设有许多箭窗。正阳门城楼和箭楼在以前是所有城楼和箭楼中最高的。

由于正阳门是各门中规格最高、位置最重要的,所以正阳门又被称为国门。门楼的三个城门,平时正中的只设不开,只有皇帝出入时才可启用。若皇帝驾崩,也不能从此门出入,因此门只进喜,不出丧,又被称为"喜门"、"吉门",皇帝结婚时可以启用。

箭楼上平时设有重兵把守,箭孔无数,并且城楼的墙上还设有火炮,以防御外敌攻城,保卫皇城的安全。然而,作为天子专用的防御外敌的国门，有一次竟然差点让当朝皇上在门前一命归天。这位皇帝就是明代的最后一位皇帝崇祯帝朱由检。据说，有一天，朱由检闲来无事，身着便装带了400名亲兵骑马朝正阳门方向前行，守门官兵因事先没有收到皇帝要来的消息，误以为是要来夺取城门的叛军，于是调转炮口便向皇帝开炮，幸亏崇祯躲得及时，才得以免遭自家大炮袭击。

每当叛军攻入北京以后，前门城楼上就会悬灯示警，以迅速报告城外的战斗情况。城楼上挂一盏灯，表示敌人已接近城下；挂两盏灯，表示战斗异常激烈；若是三盏灯，则意味着城防将要失守。崇祯皇帝就是在得知前门城楼上已悬挂三盏灯后，才被迫跑到景山上上吊自杀的。

3. 老北京系列展览

1990年、1991年，正阳门箭楼和城楼正式对外开放。站在古朴的前门城楼上，您可以尽情体验大栅栏商业街的繁华与热闹，也可以倾情领略天安门广场的庄严与神圣。同时我们还可以在正阳门城楼上参观到与老北京文化艺术、民族风情有关的系列展览，一些反映老北京平民生活的图片、照片、模型、民间工艺品等，似乎又把游客带到了几十甚至几百年前老北京的平民生活当中。另外，一些专题性的展览如摄影展、报纸展等也在此举行。

七、中山公园

1. 演变

中山公园即明清时代的社稷坛，位于天安门西侧，明永乐十八年(1420年)在元代万寿兴国寺(辽金时代的兴国寺)旧址上改建而成，是明清两代帝王祭祀土地神和五谷神的地方。1914年，开辟为中央公园；1928年，为纪念孙中山先生改名为中山公园。它面对天安门广场，与劳动人民文化宫对称，既是一座古老的园林，又是首都人民经常举行重大政治、文化活动的场所。

2. 克林德碑

步入中山公园南大门，可以看到一块汉白玉石牌坊，上书“保卫和平”四字。这块牌坊是我国人民近百年来反对帝国主义侵略压迫的见证。

1900年，八国联军入侵北京，德国公使克林德公然向义和团挑衅，被义和团团员当场打死。事后，腐败无能的清政府屈辱求和，不仅向德国赔礼道歉，还在德国公使被杀的地方建了一座“克林德坊”，立于东单的东总布胡同。1918年，第一次世界大战结束，德国战败，战胜国开会议定把“克林德碑”改为“公理战胜坊”，移至中山公园内。1952年，亚洲及太平洋区域和平会议，确定将它改为“保卫和平”坊，一直矗立于今天的中山公园内。

3. 习礼亭

在“保卫和平”牌坊的西北侧，有一六角形小亭“习礼亭”。它建于明永乐十八年(1420年)，原是明清两代专司礼仪的“鸿胪寺”里的建筑。鸿胪寺原在天安门后东侧，1900年被八国联军烧得只剩下这座习礼亭。过去，凡是初次进京朝见皇帝的官员和外国使节，都要到鸿胪寺，面对着这座习礼亭演习朝见时的礼节。1915年，习礼亭被迁至中山公园。

4. 社稷坛和中山堂

社稷坛，是中山公园内的主体建筑，在全园轴线的中心。“社”代表土地，“稷”代表谷物，此坛是皇帝专门祭祀土地之神和五谷之神的地方。坛体为三层方形坛，象征大地，上层每面长16米，中层16.8米，下层17.8米。上层台面铺五色土，分别为中黄、东青、西白、南红、北黑。据说，五色土是全国进贡来的，按道教阴阳五行之说，象征“普天之下，莫非王土”，金、木、水、火、土是万物之本。坛中央还立有一块方形石柱，名“社主石”，又称“江山石”，以示江山永固，1950年已被移去。我国古代劳动人民对社稷神非常崇拜，将其视为神灵。皇帝也会在每年春秋二、八月两次进行祭祀，以祈祷丰收。后来，遇有大火、大水、日食、天灾、出征、班师、献俘等仪式也会在这里举行。因此，“社稷”也就成了国家的象征。坛的四周有红色壝墙，四面各有一座门，以示“天子辟四门”。

社稷坛的北面是中山堂,原为社稷坛的“拜殿”,是皇帝祭祀时休息的地方。祭祀时,如果遇上雨天,便在此殿内设供桌,皇帝向南行临时祭礼,所以称为“拜殿”。这是一座木结构的大殿,白石台基,面阔五间,进深三间,建于明洪熙元年(1425年),设计上十分讲究。1925年,孙中山逝世后,曾在此停放灵柩。为了纪念这位伟人,此殿于1928年改为中山堂。以后此殿虽几经修缮,但仍然保持着明初的建筑风格。

5. 兰亭碑亭

兰亭碑亭,原建于圆明园,是圆明园的四十景之一,由一块碑和八根石柱组成,称为兰亭碑和兰亭八柱。圆明园被毁后,1917年,人们把从圆明园废址上清理出来的兰亭碑移至中山公园,而兰亭八柱则被移到了颐和园。石碑正面刻有兰亭曲水流觞图,背面则刻有清乾隆皇帝所题兰亭诗。兰亭八柱上分别刻有历代著名书法家摹写的兰亭序和兰亭诗。直到1971年初,人们才把放在颐和园的兰亭八柱移到中山公园,重新盖起了这座八角形的兰亭碑亭,并将兰亭碑置于其中,使其恢复了在圆明园中的原样。

6. 唐花坞与花展

唐花坞,坐落在中山公园的西南部,平面呈燕翅形,中部是一座八角形双檐亭,两旁是玻璃暖房。实际上,这里是一座温室花房。花房为红柱绿额,亭檐为蓝色,玲珑美观。亭的东西两端为出入口,正中一大间设喷水池,池中心安放一块高2米多的涵水石，池中喂养金鱼。花坞内陈列各种名贵花卉，1977年荷兰赠送的39个品种的郁金香，都陈列在这里。直到今天，这里每年都要举行郁金香花展，除此以外，各种应时专题花展也常在这里举行，供人们欣赏游览。

八、劳动人民文化宫

1. 演变

劳动人民文化宫旧称太庙，在故宫东侧，原是明清两代皇帝每逢重大节日以及大婚、登基、出征、班师时祭祀祖先家庙的地方。它建成于明永乐十八年(1420年)，后经过多次重修，占地面积近14万平方米，四周有三重围墙，呈南北长方形。这是北京保存最完整的古代建筑群之一，1942年被辟为和平公园，1928年成为故宫博物院的分院，但仍对游人开放。1950年5月1日，这里正式改名为“北京市劳动人民文化宫”，并新开辟了许多文化娱乐场所，如露天剧场、灯光球场、电影院、儿童体育场、小剧场、图书馆等，确实成为广大劳动人民文化活动的殿堂。另外，一年一度的春、秋季书市也在这里举行了多次，2002年已改在地坛公园。

2. 三大殿及其作用

太庙以三大殿为主体建筑。前殿为祭殿，面阔十一间，进深四间，重檐庑殿顶，有三重汉白玉石台基，四周围以石栏。大殿以前内设历代帝后牌位,牌位前有供案。两边的配殿是供奉皇族和功臣神位的地方。中殿九间,又名“寝宫”,清代在此供奉历代皇后的牌位,两边配殿贮存祭器。后殿九间,又称“祧庙”,供奉清代立国前被追封为帝、后的牌位。三大殿掩映在苍松翠柏当中,显得神秘而壮丽。

3. 中华和钟

为了迎接新世纪的到来,1999 年 11 月,以两千四百年前曾侯乙钟为原型设计的中华和钟诞生了。2000 年 1 月 1 日,江泽民总书记在太庙首先将中华和钟敲响,并且自此保存在太庙内,供游人欣赏参观。

中华和钟是由 108 只钟组成的编钟,分三层排列,高 3.8 米,宽 21 米,重达 17 吨。上层 34 个钮钟,代表我国 32 个省、自治区、直辖市和香港、澳门地区;中层 56 个甬钟代表我国 56 个民族;下层 18 个钟的中间 16 个代表中华民族的 16 个历史时期,两侧两个钟象征当今世界的主旋律“和平”与“发展”。320 公斤的中央大钟上,刻写着江泽民总书记题写的“中华和钟,万年永保”八个镏金大字。中华和钟寄托了中国人民在新世纪希望国家团结、强大和世界和平、发展的美好愿望。

九、人民大会堂

1. 简介

人民大会堂，是全国人民代表大会举行会议、共商国是的重地，是党和国家领导及人民群众重要的政治、文化活动场所。党和国家领导人经常在这里接见外国元首，进行重要的国际会晤，以发展友好往来，促进世界和平。

人民大会堂，完全由中国人自己设计，始建于1958年10月，1959年8月竣工。其南北长336米，东西宽206米，中央最高处为46.5米，建筑面积17.18万平方米，是天安门广场上最高的建筑物。

人民大会堂，主要由中部的万人大礼堂、北部的宴会大厅和南部的人大常委会办公楼三大部分组成，另外还有各种会议厅、休息厅、办公室300多个，能够满足各种会议及会晤活动的需要。

2. 廊柱

人民大会堂的周围共有廊柱134根，正门面东而开，宽83米，在5米高的台阶上，有12根擎天廊柱，内部为钢筋混凝土，外面用天然大理石镶砌而成，非常粗壮，要4人才能合抱。这八根廊柱之间的距离，中间最宽，为10.3米，次柱间距为8.2米，再往外为7.15米，其余为7米。可能很少有人知道，实际上钢筋水泥柱内芯间的距离并不是这样，中间两柱之间仅有9米，其他为7米。这样的距离看起来显得中间两柱间有点窄，于是为了避免拆毁已浇铸好的水泥廊柱，就在砌外层的包砖和大理石时特意把中间两柱的包层偏心向外移了一些，从而有了我们现在看到的视觉效果。这样一个聪明的做法在大会堂的建筑过程中节省了不少的人力物力,也体现了建筑师灵活的设计构思。

3. 中央大厅

进入大会堂的东大门，首先是中央多功能大厅。其南北长 76 米,进深 48 米,高 16 米,占地 3600 平方米，内有方柱 20 根，方柱与地面均用大理石铺砌而成,是与会者休息、活动及举行节庆娱乐活动的场所，欢迎外国元首的迎宾仪式也常在这里举行。

4. 万人大礼堂

万人大礼堂,是人民大会堂的主体建筑,采用穹庐顶,没有一根立柱支撑。大礼堂内共设三层座椅,层层递升。礼堂南北宽 76 米,东西长60 米,高 32 米,一层有座位 3693 个,二层 3515个,三层 2518 个，主席台可设座位 300～500 个，总计可容纳 1 万人。礼堂平面呈扇形，坐在任何一个位置都可以看到主席台。顶棚上分布有 500盏满天星灯,灯火齐明时真的有如满天星斗。

5. 宴会大厅

在二楼北端，是党和国家领导人举行盛大国宴和大型招待会的地方。大厅东西长 102 米,南北宽 76 米,高 15 米,面积有 7000 多平方米,可举办 5000 人的座席宴会或 10 000 人的酒会。中、西餐厨房分设于北面的东西两侧。巨大的宴会厅顶棚呈平面形,没有一根立柱支撑,也是建筑上的又一杰出力作。屋顶上的彩色藻井,充分体现了宴会厅的民族风格。

6. 各省厅

在人民大会堂的300多个会议厅、休息厅以及办公室当中，有34个是较为特别的。它们分别代表我国各个省、自治区、直辖市和香港、澳门两个特别行政区。各厅以其代表的省、自治区、直辖市和特别行政区的名字命名，并且均按照当地的民族风情、特色景物和各种特有工艺品进行装饰，充分体现了地方的文化特色。如福建厅里著名的软木雕、四川厅的竹器工艺品、陕西厅的兵马俑以及香港厅漂亮的“维多利亚港湾夜景”绒绣等等，既是各地文化的大荟萃，同时也是各地经济实力的大展示。

十、中国历史博物馆与中国革命博物馆

中国历史博物馆和中国革命博物馆，是紧紧连在一起的合成建筑物，是国庆10周年期间修建的北京十大建筑之一。其南北长313米，东西宽149米，总建筑面积为6.9万平方米。

1. 中国历史博物馆

中国历史博物馆，是我国搜集、收藏、研究和展出历史文物规模最大的博物馆，是中国最知名的历史博物馆，是浓缩了几千年悠久文明的一面明镜。该馆已有80年的历史了，1959年迁入现在的馆址，占地面积6.1万平方米。

按我国古代历史的发展过程，整个陈列被分为三个部分：第一部分从原始社会开始，通过考古发掘到的大量的珍贵文物，反映了从约170万年前到约4000年前的中国历史。第二部分是奴隶社会，它展示的是公元前21世纪到公元前476年夏、商、周、春秋这几个朝代的历史。第三部分是封建社会，它展示的是公元前475年到1840年的中国历史，反映了我国封建社会分裂与统一的更替以及最终完成统一的历史大趋势。该馆通过大量的历史文物、文献资料、图片、模型、实物等，系统、科学地展示了中华民族五千年的文明发展史，是人们了解和研究中国历史，对广大青少年进行爱国主义教育的理想场所。

现在的中国历史博物馆，将通史展览中的主要文物集中在一起，成为“珍藏特展”的主要内容。此外，“中国近代名人书法大展”、“大唐风韵——唐代社会生活展”也正在中国历史博物馆展出，感兴趣的游客不妨前去一观。

2. **中国革命博物馆**

中国革命博物馆，在北京天安门广场东侧，这个中国最驰名的“革命博物馆”建于1959年，占地8000平方米。它是一座新兴的社会主义国家博物馆，收藏了我国自1840年鸦片战争以来近代和现代的革命历史文物，是研究和宣传中国社会主义革命和建设的国家博物馆，是向人民群众宣传马列主义、毛泽东思想，进行革命传统教育的重要阵地。

中国民主主义革命时期(1840～1919)的主要陈列内容为：鸦片战争、太平天国革命运动、中法和中日战争、沙俄对中国的侵略、戊戌变法、义和团反帝运动、辛亥革命以及新的曙光八个单元。其陈列面积为1300平方米,展出文物、实物、照片和辅助展品近1000件，反映了中国人民在中国共产党成立以前反帝反封建的悲壮斗争史。

中国新民主主义革命时期(1919～1949)的主要陈列内容为：中国共产党的创建、第一和第二次国内革命战争、抗日战争以及第三次国内革命战争五个单元。其陈列面积为4000平方米,展出文物、实物、照片和辅助展品共4000余件,反映了中国人民在中国共产党的领导下,经过艰苦卓绝的奋斗,终于推翻帝国主义、封建主义和官僚资本主义在中国的统治，建立中华人民共和国的光辉历程。

该馆拥有馆藏文物10万多件、进步书刊等资料20多万册,是人们学习、了解、研究中国革命历史和进行革命传统教育的重要课堂。

近期的中国革命博物馆，由于内部建筑维修，中国旧民主主义革命时期和中国新民主主义时期的展览已停展，现正展出“我爱你，中国——共和国国旗、国徽、国歌展”和“京、津、沪、渝四市摄影联展”，游客们可以从另一个角度了解中国的革命战争史。

景 山

一、参观路线:

南门——(向东)崇祯皇帝自缢处——观妙亭——周赏亭——万春亭——(向西)富览亭——辑芳亭——(下山向东)参观绮望楼——出南门。

二、景山的地理位置及主要建筑

景山公园在北京故宫北门外，位于北京城的中轴线上。这条中轴线,南起永定门,经前门、天安门、故宫,越过景山上的万春亭,往北是地安门、鼓楼、钟楼,端正笔直。景山原是元、明、清三代封建帝王的御苑,是皇家的“禁园”,山并不高峻,但在绵延起伏的每个山峰,都建有一座不同的小亭,既一扫其“平坦无势”的缺点,又充分体现出凌空缥缈之势，成为紫禁城北面的一道屏障。景山公园内,有古老的苍松劲柏,山下有果木林，芍药园、牡丹圃，每逢花果时节，万紫千红，香飘蝶舞，一派迷人的景色。景山在明代称万岁山时，山上林木就很多，而且鹤鹿成群，山下遍布花果，称为"百果园"（或北果园），为皇帝登高、宴饮、赏花、习武射箭的地方。民国十七年（1928年），景山正式对外开放。解放后，它被辟为公园，即今天的景山公园。景山的中峰最高，达44.1米，过去是北京城内的最高点，明代建紫禁城时把这么高的一座山丘安放在帝都中心，以显示封建帝王至高无上的绝对权威，也使皇城在北面有了天然的屏障。你登山俯视，北京全景可尽收眼底。山上共有五座山峰，从东向西依次排列，每座山峰上都建有一座琉璃瓦亭，五亭中尤以主峰上的万春亭最大，东边两亭分别为周赏亭、观妙亭，西边两亭则为富览亭、辑芳亭，四亭左右对称，逐次降低。景山东麓原有一株老槐树，是李自成率领农民起义军攻入北京时，明崇祯皇帝朱由检上吊自尽的地方，现已被辟为展览室。山后的寿皇殿和观德殿，已改为北京市少年宫和少年宫图书馆，成为少年儿童学习、娱乐和进行科学活动的地方。

三、景山的形成及其名称的由来

景山的形成，是和北京城的建城史以及元、明、清三个朝代封建帝王的统治活动紧密相关的。早在800年前,这里还是一片荒郊野地。相传,金朝统治期间,在附近建造大宁宫,开凿“西华潭”(即今北海)时,曾在这里堆过一些土,形成了一个小土丘。公元13世纪,元世祖忽必烈在北京建大都城,因这里正处城内的中心地区,南逼大门,于是就在这里开辟了专供皇帝赏乐的“后苑”。当时苑内原有的小土丘,已经芳草菲菲,称作“青山”,这就是今天景山的前身。

明永乐十四年(1416年)为了营建紫禁城宫殿,工匠们就将拆除元代旧城和挖掘紫禁城护城河的淤泥、渣土,就近堆积在原来的小土丘上,这样就逐渐形成了今天的五座山峰,取名“万岁山”。因为它成为紫禁城背后的“天然屏障”,所以明清两朝都把它当做宫廷的“镇山”,藉以维护他们的统治地位。据说,明成祖朱棣营建北京宫殿时,曾在山下堆存用煤,所以景山又被俗称为煤山。

清顺治十二年(1655年),万岁山更名为景山,成为皇帝举行一些祭祀活动的地方。“景”是高大的意思,《诗·殷武》中有“陡坡景山,松柏丸丸”之句,说的是商朝的都城有一座景山,人们登上山来,一边欣赏着山上的美景,一边赞美松柏长的高大茂盛。全诗是为了歌颂商代帝王武丁在商朝的统治濒于危急的时刻,消灭灾难祸乱,从而带来王室中兴的丰功伟绩。人们采景山上的松柏为他建造宗庙,岁时祭祀,带有永思、追远的含义。清初,顺治把万岁山改叫景山,希望清朝能够居安思危，以求统治的长治久安。

四、绮望楼

故宫神武门的对面是景山公园的正南门，名北上门。入北上门,迎面是一幢绮望楼。它依山就势,形制精巧,给人以先声夺人之感。这里原是乾隆皇帝办官学时用以供奉孔子牌位的地方。北上门左右的房屋,就是当时教导内务府子弟读书的书房,现在已被改成展览室,经常举办绘画、陶瓷、书法等艺术展览。楼后便是景山山麓,登山道旁边布满春花秋菊,艳丽多彩。

五、景山上的五亭

万春亭

富览亭　　　　周赏亭

辑芳亭　　　　　　观妙亭

前面已经介绍,景山上有五座山峰,每一峰上都建有一座形式精巧的琉璃瓦亭子。这五座亭子于乾隆十五年(1751年),依山就势,在五个山峰上建造而成。中峰上的叫万春亭,是景山上的至高点；西侧的叫富览亭，东侧的叫周赏亭；再往东西分别是重檐圆形蓝瓦亭，东边叫观妙亭,西边叫辑芳亭,四亭左右对称。当时每座亭内都有一尊象征性的铜铸神像,代表酸、甜、苦、辣、咸五种味道，所以又被称为“五味神”。1900年，八国联军入侵北京，两侧四亭内的铜像都被抢去，只有万春亭里的一尊得以保存下来，但也被砍断了一只左臂。游人登上景山的万春亭后，可以一览整个北京城的盛景，气势非常壮观。

六、万春亭上鸟瞰京城

登景山，从东、西两麓都可到达中峰。站在万春亭里，可以饱览山上、山下以及周围的壮丽景色。

北望，可以看到笔直的地安门大街。鼓楼雄峙大街的北端，像一条玉带的一端镶嵌着一块巨大的宝珠。靠景山的这一端，大街两旁矗立着几座雄伟的新建筑，民族形式的屋顶覆盖着绿色琉璃瓦，和景山宫殿的黄色琉璃瓦顶，构成统一和谐的格局。

转向西南，园中一派南国的秀丽景色。什刹海隔一条马路和北海相连。这儿山明水净，湖岸上游人如鲫，湖中轻舟慢摇，鸽群带着哨声，在琼岛上空绕着白塔飞翔，胜似太液晴空。

在万春亭的南面，北京的整个布局看得一清二楚，一条纵贯全城的中轴线，分外明显。许多重要的古典建筑，在中轴线上分布得十分对称。如太庙(劳动人民文化宫)和社稷坛(中山公园)分布于中轴线的两侧；中部故宫的一片片金黄色的琉璃瓦殿顶，在阳光的照耀下，金光闪闪，周围的绿色松柏如同大海，好像座座龙宫宝殿浮出水面，美不胜收。故宫的前面，天安门到前门之间，是中国首都北京的中心广场——天安门广场。

如果是早晨，逆光东望，东单王府井繁华的商业街上，近几年新建的一批现代化宾馆、饭店，矗立霞光中，隐约可见，又是另一番现代都市的壮丽景观。

七、明崇祯帝自缢处

从中峰走景山的东麓，在观妙亭东侧的山坡上，你可以看见一株向东倾斜的老槐树，其四周有围栏围绕，这就是明朝末代皇帝崇祯帝朱由检上吊自尽的地方。原来的老槐树，用锁链锁住，被称为“罪槐”，八国联军攻入北京时，将锁链掠走了。后来人们又在周围加筑矮墙维护，前面立碑，上面写着“明思宗殉国处”。但是，这些都在十年文化大革命期间遭到破坏，老槐树也被砍去了。现在游客们看到的老槐树，是后来补栽上去的。

崇祯皇帝在此处自缢身亡，当时也是不得以的事情。明崇祯十七年(1644年)三月十七日，李自成率领农民起义军攻入北京，炮击北京城，城外的明军纷纷投降。十八日，阜成、西便二门的守军也开门迎接起义军入城。皇宫中的崇祯皇帝本想骑马从紫禁城的南门逃出去，但纷乱之中，堂堂的一国之君竟被挡在平日自己进出自如的城门之内。无奈之下,朱由检只得又折而向北，返回宫中。匆忙中，他剑刺公主，逼死皇后，然后丢冠散发，身着白色暗龙长袍，脚穿一双从秉笔太监王承恩那里换来的软底鞋，于次日凌晨,狼狈地爬上了景山。他徘徊观望一阵见已无可挽回之后,便吊死在一棵老槐树上。据说他临死之前，还叹着气说：“我平日待臣下也不薄,今日落到这步田地,群臣中竟没有一个来跟我一起尽节！”说罢,便走下山坡，把腰带解下来,在老槐树下“以身殉国”了。

景山之所以有名,在很大程度上,就是因为这个亡国之君曾在此处自缢身亡的缘故。清嘉庆年间有人作诗云:“巍巍万岁山,密密接烟树,中有望帝魂，悲啼不知处”，用以吊念这位末世君主。

八、寿皇殿和观德堂

现在的寿皇殿,是乾隆十四年(1749年)把明代建在东北部的寿皇殿移建到中峰的后面(即现在的地方),并进行扩建的结果。扩建后的这组建筑有正殿、左右山殿、东西配殿以及神厨、神库、碑亭、井亭等附属建筑。正殿九间的前边有戟门,正门还有琉璃坊和石狮,在苑内自成一局,显得辉煌肃穆。原来正殿供奉康熙的“神御”,后来这里成为专门供奉皇室祖先影像的地方。另外，自清顺治开始，皇帝的灵柩（称“梓宫”）以及待用的空棺材，也都放在这里。

今天的寿皇殿已改为“北京少年宫”，成为北京少年儿童的乐园。

观德堂，在寿皇殿以东，是明代皇室练武用的“射箭所”，以后也改作皇帝停放棺椁之用。

九、关帝庙

过去，景山的后面有一座关帝庙，里面供奉着“关公立马像”。关公，原是三国时蜀国的一名大将，名关羽。宋代以前，关公的影响并不太大，自宋以后，才名声大震。明代他被加封为关帝，后更有“武圣人”之称，与“文圣人”孔子并立。在民间，百姓认为关公具有司命禄、佑科举、治病除灾、驱邪避恶、巡祭冥司乃至招财进宝、庇护商贾等多种法力，所以民间各行各业，妇孺长幼，都对这样一位万能神十分敬重，并立庙供奉。又因历史上的关公是一位忠贞不二的英雄好汉，历代统治者也愿意用“忠孝节义”集于一身的关羽来教化臣民，维护封建统治秩序。到了清朝，皇帝仍然对关公推崇备至，将其奉为“护国之神”。景山后的这座关帝庙，当然也有统治者要借助关羽威名，保佑帝国长治久安的意思。因此，此庙的正式名称定为“护国忠义庙”。

十、景山与北京大学

几十年前，景山曾一度改为北京大学的校园。那时景山东门正对着马神庙街,北大文、理、法三个学院的男生大部分住在马神庙西口的“西斋”，女生住在嵩公府夹道进去的“天、地、玄、黄”等新楼。距离都不远。大概是民国时期，决定把景山辟为公园，北大便又迁走了。解放后，景山被列为北京市重点文物保护单位，多次进行修缮，铺设道路，进行大面积的绿化，种植果树，栽培花卉，成为广大人民喜爱的公园之一。

北 海

一、参观路线

整个北海的参观游览，大致可以划分成两部分：

1. 琼岛景区：进南门——团城——过永安桥到永安寺——白塔——从西北面下山参观悦

心殿——庆霄楼——阅古楼——铜仙人承露盘——琼岛春阴碑。

2. 北海沿岸景观：北海沿岸有东门、北门、西门，从任何一门进入后沿岸参观均可。西岸到东岸的景观布局大致如下：西门——西岸北海校场碑——万佛楼石碑——北岸五龙亭——铁影壁——九龙壁——静心斋——西天梵境（天王殿）——先蚕坛——北门——东岸画舫斋——濠濮间——东门。

二、概况

出故宫博物院的北门，向西走约500米，便来到北海公园。这里原是皇家园林，禁止百姓随意观瞻。全园占地面积70多万平方米，其中水面占50%以上。从辽代起，金、元、明、清几个朝代均在此修建皇家御苑。辽代，此处原是一片湖泊沼泽，后来建造了瑶屿行宫。据传，其最高处的殿宇，曾有辽萧太后的梳妆台。金灭辽后，挖湖堆土，砌石成山，先后建琼华岛、瑶光殿、广寒殿等，并从河南开封运来宋代艮岳的太湖石，使其成为金朝皇帝在中都郊外的行宫——大宁宫（1179年建成）。1260年，元世祖忽必烈迁都，以琼华岛、太液池为中心，大兴土木，建造大都新城，并将琼华岛改名万寿山（后又改为万岁山）。明代，将太液池分为两个部分，后又开凿南端小湖，故而形成北海、中海和南海。明清两代，在三海沿岸相继建造起许多殿宇楼阁、亭台水榭。清初顺治八年(1651年),人们又在广寒殿旧址上建造藏式白塔,并将万寿山易名为白塔山。此时的太液池、琼华岛已建成皇城内规模最大、风景最优美的皇家御苑。1900年,八国联军侵占北京时,这里是日、法、俄的联合司令部,北海几度成为废墟。1902年,慈禧再度修复御苑,并作为她本人的"颐养"之地。直到1925年,北海才向广大公众开放,从而结束了它作为皇家御苑的历史。

三、团城

1. 简介

团城,在北海公园南门西侧,是一座圆台式的古老园林建筑,已有八百多年的历史。早在辽代,这里是瑶屿(琼华岛)南边的另一个小岛,俗称"圆坻"。金朝时期,这个小岛是大宁宫建筑的一部分。元世祖忽必烈以太液池为中心建造大都城时,便在金时旧址上建造了"仪天殿",并在岛的四周拓成一座圆台,建起石城。明永乐年间,在岛的周围用砖筑起了城墙,重修仪天殿(1417年),改名为"承光殿",后又称为"乾光殿"(1552年)。清康熙八年(1669年),北京发生地震,团城遭到破坏。后来,人们对团城进行了大规模的修建,1746年,乾光殿修复成功,仍改叫"承光殿"。

团城，是历代帝王的御园，周长276米，面积4550平方米，城墙高4.6米，四周筑有城堞垛墙。团城以承光殿和玉瓮亭为主体建筑，整个建筑，玲珑精巧，轻盈秀丽，在古园林建筑中别具一格。它两面临水，是琼华岛的影照，又宛如镶嵌在玉盘中的一颗明珠。团城东西两面辟有城门，东为昭景门，西为衍祥门。1900年，八国联军入侵北京时，曾破坏衍祥门，解放后（1953年）重新修复。现在的团城北面，根据周总理生前的指示，筑有一道台阶，便于游人直接从北海登上团城游览。同时，这里还经常举办工艺美术等各种展览。

2. 承光殿

承光殿，是团城上最主要的建筑。它建在八角形的台基上，重檐飞脊，为一座12间的八角殿。四面推出的抱厦为单檐卷棚式，黄瓦绿剪边，形式独特，造型优美，是我国古代建筑中罕见的。走进大殿，在四根巨大的井口柱上，有清咸丰皇帝的御笔所题：南面为“九陌红尘飞不到，十洲清风晓来多”；北面为“七宝庄严开玉镜，万年福寿护金瓯”。上悬匾额是那拉氏慈禧亲笔题写的“大圆宝镜”。殿内正中是一尊用整块白玉雕刻而成的佛像，为释迦牟尼坐像，高1.5米，全身洁白无瑕，清润光泽，雕琢艺术极高。玉佛全身披挂袈裟，头顶和衣褶都镶嵌着红绿各色的小宝石，堪为稀世之珍。这尊玉佛，相传是清光绪二十三年（1897年），北京僧人明宽游历南洋时,从缅甸募化而来,进献给慈禧的。慈禧将它供奉在团城承光殿。可惜在玉佛的左臂上,留下一道深深的刀痕,这是1900年八国联军侵略者毁坏文物的见证。

3. 遮荫侯

承光殿东侧,有一棵金代种植的栝子松,树冠如盖,雄伟挺拔,距今已有八百多年的历史,清乾隆皇帝曾封之为“遮荫侯”,是园中古树的精品。

4. 玉瓮亭

承光殿前方有座蓝顶白柱的玉瓮亭,亭内中央汉白玉石莲座上安放着一个黑色大钵盂,由一整块巨型墨玉雕琢而成。亭高70厘米,直径1.5米,周长约5米,重约3500公斤。外壁刻有鱼龙海兽,出入于波涛之中,形象十分生动。据传,1265年此物曾放在广寒殿里(白塔山顶),称为“渎山大玉海”,是元世祖忽必烈大宴群臣时盛酒用的玉瓮。明朝时广寒殿倒塌拆除,玉瓮流落到西华门外真武庙。庙内道士起初用它做菜缸,后来得知是珍品,才放入殿堂内。1749年,乾隆用一千两银子把玉钵买来,并专门在团城上建亭放置它。乾隆认为玉钵名称不甚雅观,又赐名为“玉瓮”,并亲笔题写了“御制玉瓮歌”,刻在玉瓮膛内。另外,亭四角的方柱上,也刻有内廷翰林等人所作的诗词。据说这块大型墨玉很可能来自我国四川西部的岷山,因为那里过去曾叫“渎山”。

四、琼华岛

1. 琼华岛

琼华岛，位于北海整个水域的东南角，辽代名瑶屿，建有行宫；金代时，改称琼华岛，属万宁宫的一部分；元代为万寿山；清顺治时称白塔山。岛高 45 米，绕岛一周约 900 米。从琼华岛到白塔山，虽然历经数百年的变迁，但始终保持了神海仙山、海市蜃楼的意境。整个琼华岛建筑中轴线吻合于主峰中轴线，主峰极点亦是南北、东西两条轴线的正交点，从而十分鲜明地突出了白塔，显示了封建王朝的君神一致和至高无上。从北宋御花园运来的太湖石，点缀在琼华岛的山前山后，组成峰、峦、峭壁、谷道、台、沟壑以及变幻莫测的假山洞，突出了仙山楼阁的境界。岛南部矗立着主体建筑永安寺；岛东侧有见春亭、古遗堂、看画廊和交翠亭；岛北面有紫翠房、嵌岩室、环碧楼和盘岚精舍等；岛西面的亩鉴室、酣古堂和写妙石室等，都缀有假山，忽而山峰，忽而峭壁，忽而山洞，忽广忽狭，变化无穷。在法轮殿北侧，有两块奇特的石头，上面刻有乾隆皇帝御笔题写的“昆崙”两字以及三首诗。整个琼华岛四面都有石梯山路可以到达山顶，东、南面有石桥和岸边相连，并与岸边秀丽的景色交相辉映，构成一幅壮丽的画卷。

2. **永安寺**

永安寺，位于琼华岛南部，走进北海大门，从团城过永安桥，便可到永安寺山门。永安桥是用汉白玉砌成的石桥，建于13世纪，是连接琼华岛和团城的纽带。桥的南北两端各有牌坊一座，北为“堆云”，南叫“积翠”，故而又称“堆云积翠”桥。牌坊两侧各有一对石狮分列左右。永安寺是清顺治八年(1651年)，在明代仁智、介福、延和三大殿的旧址上建造的。从永安寺到白塔，正是琼华岛的中轴线。永安寺原称白塔寺，乾隆八年(1743年)才易为现名。从山脚下拾级而上，法轮殿、正觉殿、普安殿和善因殿依山就势排列，直到白塔，形成一座完整的西藏密宗黄教喇嘛寺庙。

3. **白塔**

白塔，在琼华岛的山顶，是琼华岛最突出的建筑。它始建于清顺治八年(1651年)，康熙、雍正年间因地震塌毁，先后两次重修。新中国建立后，也经过多次重修，才基本恢复原貌。

白塔为喇嘛塔，塔身呈宝瓶形，下面为高大的砖石台基，塔座为折角式须弥座，通高35.9米。塔身上部为两层铜质伞盖，边缘悬挂铜钟十四个，最上为镏金火焰宝珠塔刹。塔南有一座用琉璃砖砌成的善因殿，殿中央供有文殊菩萨化身的铜像，俗称“镇海佛”，四壁雕刻有千手千眼佛像。据记载：当年，佛事的规模做得很大，每年旧历十月二十五日，从山下点灯，直达塔顶，塔光罗列，恍若星斗。一群喇嘛吹吹打打，深夜方休，以祈福迎祥。在白塔北面，曾经立有5根刹竿，俗称“五虎刹竿”，专为防变所用。遇到紧急情况，白天升龙旗，黑夜挂灯笼。各方向颜色不同，东蓝、西白、南红、北黑，黄色在城中。如果敌人白天从东西两面进攻，则五虎刹竿上升起蓝色和白色两种龙旗，城内八旗看到信号，立即集合队伍，分东西两面迎敌。因此，这里又有向城中示警的作用。

4. **悦心殿**

悦心殿，在琼华岛西部山坡上。乾隆三十八年(1773年)修建。从那时起，乾隆、嘉庆、道光、咸丰、同治、光绪历代帝王游赏北海时，都要在此殿临时听政和接见大臣。院中还有专供帝王品茶和用早点的御茶房和饽饽房。

5. **庆霄楼**

绕过悦心殿便是庆霄楼。其楼宇高耸，大有可冲霄汉之势。自乾隆起，皇帝每年腊月都要陪其母坐在楼内，燃起火炉，观看北海冰面上的“冰嬉”活动。“冰嬉”，就是在冰上掷球的一种游戏，是那时冬天人们的一项主要娱乐活动。

6. **阅古楼**

阅古楼，在琼岛西北面山坡脚下，建于清乾隆十八年(1753年)。阅古楼依山面水，整齐为半月形，左右环抱，分上下两层，各五间。楼梯为螺旋式，称“蟠龙升天”。匾额上“阅古楼”三字为清乾隆皇帝御笔亲书。楼内上层壁间嵌满乾隆年间摹刻的《三希堂法帖》,共495方,是我国现存最完整的书法艺术石刻珍品，汇集了我国书法艺术中的精华。“三希堂”是故宫养心殿西侧的一间小屋子,本是清代皇帝的私人藏书屋。乾隆曾将三位晋朝大书法家的手迹即王羲之的《快雪时晴帖》、王献之的《中秋帖》、王珣的《伯远帖》,收藏在这里,故而此屋被称为“三希堂”。乾隆十二年(1747年),特令梁诗正等人,将内府所藏魏、晋及历代的名家手迹编汇成《三希堂石渠宝籍法帖》32卷,请了上等刻工,刻于石板,又将石板嵌入阅古楼墙壁。这部“法帖”共收集我国明末以前134人的340件作品,并有题跋210多件,约9万字,是我国书法艺术的荟萃。现在的阅古楼已成为广大书法爱好者游览和学习的地方。

7. 铜仙人承露盘

在琼岛北侧山腰处，有一根高达4.5米的汉白玉蟠龙石柱,石柱上有一铜制古装人像,双手高托一只荷花形大铜盘，俗称“铜仙人承露盘”。相传，汉武帝刘彻妄想长生，信奉神仙道教。一个道士说,用天降的露水搅拌玉石的碎屑一齐服用，可使人止住阴气，永生阳气，达到长生不老。于是,刘彻下令在长安建章宫,修建一个铜仙人承露盘,以求长生不老。这只铜仙人承露盘，就是乾隆皇帝仿汉武帝求仙的故事建造的。但它的真正作用是用来点缀景色的,并不是用来承接露水,以求长生不老的。

8. 琼岛春阴

琼岛春阴位于琼岛东北面。1761年，清乾隆皇帝游览琼华岛时触景生情，亲笔书写“琼岛春阴”四字，立碑于绿阴深处，这里遂成为著名的燕京八景之一。碑身呈四方形，碑文周围框刻有缠枝莲花装饰。碑座四周有雕刻精致的石护栏。燕京，即北京的别称。八景之名，最早始于金代，指北京著名的八处名胜古迹。清朝乾隆年间，乾隆亲自题字制成八块石碑，分别立在燕京八景所在地。这八景分别是：居庸关长城的居庸叠翠、德胜门外西北的蓟门烟树、卢沟桥的卢沟晓月、玉泉山的玉泉垂虹、香山香雾窟的西山晴雪、北海琼岛的琼岛春阴、中南海水榭的太液秋风、日坛南坛的金台夕照。

五、北海沿岸景观

西岸

1. 北海教场碑

1752年，乾隆帝在西苑设教场（今北海中学内），用以训练八旗军队，并篆文立碑以训后世。1999年，国家为保护文物，将北海教场碑立在北海西岸，供游客观赏。

2. 万佛楼石碑

石碑位于北海公园内的原万佛楼前，是乾隆皇帝为庆祝母亲的80岁大寿而建，因楼内供有万尊金质佛像而得名。1900年，八国联军入侵北京，佛像被抢掠一空。现在，万佛楼已荡然无存,仅存一块万佛楼石碑。这块石碑,立于乾隆三十五年(1770年),碑的四面分别刻有汉、满、蒙古、藏四种文字的《万佛楼落成瞻礼诗》。1987年石碑移立于此,以示纪念。

北岸

1. 五龙亭

五龙亭,位于北海北岸西部,铁影壁南侧。此亭建于明万历三十年(1602年),原是明代泰素殿旧址,殿中有草亭。清顺治八年(1651年),拆毁原来的泰素殿,改建成五龙亭。这里是明清两代皇帝在湖边垂钓和观看焰火的地方。中间最大的一座重檐亭子叫龙泽亭,东为澄祥亭、滋香亭;西为涌瑞亭、浮翠亭,五亭之间由桥和汉白玉栏杆左右曲折相连,如同一条巨龙在湖面上蜿蜒腾跃,所以将这五座亭子合称为五龙亭。其中龙泽、滋香、浮翠三亭石岸下,各有一单孔石桥通向北岸。五龙亭又称天地亭,按照天圆地方的说法,龙泽亭为圆形,属天象,只有皇帝才能在这里垂钓、赏月、观看焰火。东西两侧的亭子为方形,属地象,是王妃、文武大臣陪同游宴的地方。

2. 铁影壁

铁影壁,位于北海北岸,雕造于元代,壁高1.89米,檐口长3.56米。壁通身为暗紫色,看上去好像用铁铸成一样,所以被称为铁影壁。实际上,这是由一块暗紫色的中性火成岩雕刻而成。影壁的檐顶上有脊吻瓦檐，檐下两面均刻有奇兽祥云等，还有古代人们心目中象征“吉祥”的动物——狻猊。这座铁影壁和地安门的金门墩、东安门外的银闸、新街口北大街的铜井、太液池北岸的锡殿，共称为北京的金银铜铁锡五大古迹。不过，现在仅存这座铁影壁了。

3. 九龙壁

九龙壁，位于铁影壁北侧，建于清乾隆二十一年(1756年)。壁高6.65米，厚1.42米，长26米，是一座全部用彩色琉璃砖砌成的影壁。底座为青白玉石台基，上有绿琉璃须弥座。前后两面各有九条蟠龙，戏珠于汹涌的波涛和飘浮云朵的天空之间，造型活泼，姿态各异，栩栩如生。影壁的东端嵌有海水、流云和旭日东升，西端嵌有海水、流云和明月当空。壁的正脊、垂脊、筒瓦等处都嵌有龙，总共有635条之多。皇帝是真龙天子，属九五之尊，因此，九龙壁规格最高。全国现存九龙壁三座：一座在山西大同，它建于明永乐年间，是修建时间最早的；一座在故宫皇极门前，工艺最为精美；北海这座，因其两面均刻有九龙，最有特色，是驰名中外的古代琉璃建筑艺术的珍品。

4. 静心斋

静心斋，位于太液池北岸，原名镜清斋，建于乾隆二十二年(1757年)，1913年改称此名。这是北海古建筑中保存最完整、最精美的一处行宫小园。静心斋东枕山，西倚寺，正门与琼岛隔水相望，四周以矮墙围绕，南面为透空花墙，内外景色交融，呈现一片宁静、祥和的气氛。其东西长约110米，南北进深约45米，占地面积约4800平方米。此处，原是乾隆皇帝游乐读书的地方，又称“乾隆小花园”。后来，这里又成为清代皇太子读书之所，也是清代帝王后妃去大西天拈香拜佛时暂时休息的行宫。1900年，八国联军侵占北京时，日本侵略军的司令部就设在静心斋，该斋遂惨遭破坏。1931年，这里曾是北洋政府宴请外国主子的地方。新中国成立后，经过全面整修，静心斋才恢复了过去的秀美与绮丽。

全园建筑分隔为几个大小不同的院落，环环相套，层层进深。院内有一莲池，迎面就是主体建筑镜清斋，其主景区是北面横架水面的沁泉廊，站在廊内可以环眺全园景色。廊东端是一座精巧的汉白玉石桥，俗称小玉带桥。桥南是一个雅致的小院，院内水池止水如镜。东面是韵琴斋，北面为抱素书屋，疏竹明窗，是清皇太子的读书处。沁泉廊之西，是一座用太湖石堆成的假山，山上有一被乾隆誉为莲朵珠宫的枕峦亭。亭西北隅的叠翠楼，是园中之园静心斋内的最高建筑，蹬楼远眺，太液池琼华岛的无限风光美景，尽收眼底。

5. 西天梵境

静心斋往西是“西天梵境”。这里原是明代西天禅林喇嘛庙，清代(1759年)重修，是翻译和印刷大藏经的地方。山门外，建有一座精美的琉璃牌坊，牌坊南额为“华藏界”，北额为“须弥春”。它有一姐妹牌坊，是圆明园的“慈云普护”牌坊，1860年毁于英法联军之手。山门内有两块著名的石碑，左边刻有全部的金刚经，右边雕着全部的药师经。西天梵境的正殿为“大慈真如宝殿”，是明代建筑的一座楠木结构的殿堂，这在北京城内是很少见的。宝殿内供奉三尊5米高的大铜佛，俗名三世佛。大慈真如宝殿前有天王殿，后面是两层的琉璃阁，称为大琉璃宝殿。匾额上题有“华严清界”四字，旁边刻有回文。在殿外的琉璃壁上嵌砌五彩花饰和许多小佛像，精美异常，所以这里又有“万佛殿”之称。1900年，八国联军侵略者将宫内珍宝抢掠一空。

6. 先蚕坛

先蚕坛，是北海北岸的一座碧瓦红墙大院，也称“蚕坛”，建于1742年，是北京九坛之一。坛体呈方形，周长530多米，东西北三面植满护坛桑林，正面是亲蚕殿，殿前是先蚕坛和瘗坎坛，南面是观桑台。殿后是洗蚕池，一直通到东侧的洗蚕河，河上有木桥两座，南桥偏东是西陵氏神殿，北桥东侧是蚕所。先蚕坛是清代后妃们每年祭祀蚕神的地方。现在先蚕坛周围，设有蚕坛饭店和儿童游乐场，供游人餐饮娱乐之用。

东岸

1. 画舫斋

画舫斋又称水殿，在北海东岸，为清乾隆二

十二年(1757年)所建,是清朝皇家行宫之一,总称“春雨林塘”,正殿叫画舫斋。清代皇帝常约著名画家到此作画,所创作品也在此陈列。画舫斋内是厅廊环抱水池所组成的四合院封闭空间,既有北方庭院建筑特点,又有江南园林风格。画舫斋建在水上,仿佛一只浮在水上的大船,故而得名。它的西北有一座与曲折的走廊相连的小院,叫“小玲珑”。慈禧的烟房设在这里,有时赌场也设在此处。东北院有“古柯庭”,庭前立着一棵直径4米、同殿檐一般高的古老槐树,相传为唐代遗物,俗称“唐槐”。据传,门外是检阅射箭的地方,每年春末夏初之交,清帝的亲王、君王、王公大臣等都来登场赛箭,胜者有赏。1900年,八国联军侵占北京时,法国侵略军司令部就设在画舫斋。现在,这里经常兴办美术、摄影等各种展览,参观者总是络绎不绝。

2. 濠濮间

濠濮间也在北海东岸,位于画舫斋的南面。相传乾隆游巡江南时,带来了描绘图本,于1757年依图仿建。濠濮间是清代皇宫宴请大臣的地方。它的中心建筑是一座水榭,东西北三面临水,四周山石环绕,游赏此处既可耳闻林中鸟语,又可眼观水中游鱼,绿茵遍及山坡之上,别有一番自然风趣。濠濮间的水池上有一座雕栏九曲石桥,桥北端有一座石牌坊,两面均有对联一副,主要描绘了园内山水松竹如诗如画的动态。夏季,慈禧常在这里消夏避暑,听艺人说评书,有时还和嫔妃们投壶聚赌。

北海公园是我国园林艺术的珍品，除了上述介绍的景点之外，还有很多地方值得驻足游览观赏,相信只要您踏入这里,就一定会为她的自然天成与人工雕琢的完美结合而折服。

现代都市风情

现在的北京不仅是驰名中外的历史名城,同时也是高度发展的现代化大都市。天安门广场、故宫、景山、北海,坐落于北京的中心,传统文化的含蓄与凝重蕴含其中；周边则是现代化的高楼大厦，现代大都市的开放与张扬宣示其外。游览北京,既要了解它的过去,也要熟悉其现在。让我们从传统文化中走出来,去领略一下北京这座现代都市的风情吧!

一、西单文化广场

从天安门沿长安街往西到西单路口东北侧，便是有名的西单文化广场。它占地面积约2.16万平方米,建筑面积3.5万平方米。广场上绿茵满地，常年布置各种各样的花雕、装饰、雕塑，人们可以在绿地旁的路椅上休憩聊天，尽情领略闹市中那份独有的绿洲风情。

整个广场分为地上地下两大部分：地上的文化广场，中心部分凹陷，四周墙壁上设有科普画廊和西单地区有历史风味的浮雕，充满了文化气息。地下是两层的商务、娱乐活动区域，与西单地铁站相通，里面有商场、餐厅、电影院、游泳池、溜冰场、壁球场等相应配套设施，是集休闲、娱乐、购物于一体的大众文化活动场所。

二、北京图书大厦

北京图书大厦，位于西单文化广场东侧，是中国最大的书店。大厦于 1998 年 5 月 18 日正式开业，建筑面积 5 万多平方米，地下 3 层，地上 8 层，是目前北京及全国最大的现代化图书商城。1999 年 3 月 9 日，这里还开设了网上书店，有 50 万种图书可供每年 100 万访问者及购书者选择。习惯于网上购物的朋友，不用出门就可在网上选购到自己称心如意的书籍。

三、西单商业街

西单商业街，是西单地区最为繁华热闹的地区。该地区商店林立，散发着浓烈的现代商业气息。这里的主要商厦有西单商场、购物中心、华威大厦、西单赛特、中友百货等。现在的西单商业街，东有文化广场，西有中银大厦，路口对面是首都时代广场，已经成为仅次于王府井的北京第二条现代化商业大街。

四、中国银行总行大厦

中国银行总行大厦，位于西单十字路口西北角，外形好像一只巨大的首饰盒。大厦由中国银行主建，总投资达22亿元人民币，建筑面积17.4万平方米。大厦地下4层，地上15层，内设银行营业大厅、外汇交易厅、银行写字楼、会议室、外宾接待厅、报告厅、金库、保管箱库、食堂、地下车库等，是一座多功能的智能型管理大厦。

五、首都时代广场

首都时代广场，位于西单十字路口东南角，1998～1999年，由西单商业区建设开发公司与九龙仓储集团北京有限公司合资兴建，总投资20亿元，占地2.31公顷，建筑面积20多万平方米。它由A、B两区组成，地下设2层。A区地上1～3层为商场，4～14层为写字楼；B区地上1～3层为商场。2002年12月12日，首都时代广场与地铁通道开通，位于时代广场的地下二层，正好把西单东南商业区与北侧商业区紧密连接起来,促进了西单商业街的繁荣和发展。首都时代广场是集办公、商业、酒店和公寓于一体的综合性建筑。

六、前门大街

前门大街，在元、明、清时代就是著名的商业街，现在与王府井大街、西单北大街，并列为北京著名的三条传统商业大街。这条大街始建于元代，明清时期是达官显贵及各地来京人士喜爱光顾的地方，也是距离内城禁地最近的商业街。它北起前门(正阳门),南至永定门,长约2公里,其中尤以北面的大栅栏一带最为热闹,老北京的商业气氛最浓。老北京的一些有名的老字号都可以在这里找到，如开业于1893年的瑞蚨祥绸缎店、诞生于1669年的同仁堂药店、始创于明代嘉靖九年（1530年）的六必居酱菜园，以及享誉京城的全聚德烤鸭、都一处烧麦等。可以说，前门大街是了解老北京风情的一个极好去处。

七、王府井大街

王府井大街,是北京最著名的商业大街,有“金街”之称。早在七百多年前的元代,这里就是众多官府机构和王府聚居的地方，明清时已发展为一条比较繁华的商业街了。由于过去这条街上曾有一口甜水井，所以被称为“王府井”。王府井大街由南到北有1600多米，以前街道狭窄，有碍于现代都市的发展，因而在北京市政府的批准下，对王府井大街进行了改造。改造后的王府井大街上的主要建筑有东方广场、北京饭店、工美大厦、好友世界、新东安市场、百货大楼、东堂（天主教堂）、天元利生体育商厦、天伦王朝饭店、国际艺苑皇冠假日饭店、王府井饭店、首都剧场、华侨大厦等。另外，街头还辟有绿地、花坛、喷泉、座椅等，供游人休憩、娱乐。在附近还有京城著名的夜市风味小吃一条街，来到这里，您几乎可以品尝到京城每一种特色小吃。

八、北京饭店

北京饭店，位于王府井大街南口西侧，是北京最古老而又最具时代特色的老字号饭店。它由三大部分组成，分别反映了北京饭店经历的不同时代：中楼，浅米色，7层，高40米，有客房140多间，1917年由法国人修建，体现了典型的欧洲风格，是北京出现最早、最高级的大型饭店；中西楼，深褐色，8层，高44米，采用中国的传统建筑风格，有客房240多间，是新中国成立初，于1954年建立的高级饭店，内设宫殿式的豪华大宴会厅，当年周总理曾在此举行盛大的招待会；东楼，黄橙色，23层，高89米，有客房

600 多间,兴建于 1974 年,是一座现代化的高层建筑。

九、贵宾楼饭店

位于北京饭店西侧,是一座橙红色建筑,共10层,高 41 米,内设总统套房及高级客房 287 间,于 1989 年由北京饭店集团和香港知名人士霍英东先生合资兴建,是一座兼容中西方建筑风格的现代化豪华旅游饭店。

十、东方广场

东方广场,位于王府井大街南口东侧,动工兴建于 1997 年,于 2000 年全部竣工。它占地面积近 11 万平方米,建筑面积达 90 万平方米,总投资 19.438 亿美元。这项工程是由北京鸿联文化有限责任公司与以李嘉诚、董建成先生为首的香港汇贤投资有限公司共同合作兴建的。广场共分 13 段、13 座楼宇,是一座集商业、服务、娱乐、写字楼、公寓及五星级饭店为一体的建筑群。广场地下设有“古人类遗址博物馆”,是在东方广场施工开挖地基时发现的。东方广场西面是北京金街王府井大街,东面是北京银街东单北大街,南面是神州第一街长安街,占有极优越的地理位置,已与王府井、东单北大街一起成为北京最著名的国际性商业中心和亚洲最庞大的商务建筑群体。

十一、东单北大街

东单之名始于明清时期，因此处原是长安街东端，并且立有一座单数牌楼，所以有“东单”之称。现在的东单北大街长约 1600 多米，开设有很多以经营进口服装类商品为主的专卖店，如苹果、鳄鱼、金利来、罗宾汉、百图、麋老大等，可称得上是专卖店一条街。同时，此街的配套设施也不错，购物、餐饮、娱乐等，应有尽有，是陪好友逛街的好去处。

游览须知

一、天安门城楼

1. 联系电话:(010)63095745

2. 开放时间: 8: 00～17: 00(16: 30停止售票)

3. 票价:成人每人15元,学生每人5元

二、毛主席纪念堂

1. 联系电话:(010)65132277

2. 开放时间:

星期二至星期日　上午 8: 30～11: 30

星期二和星期四　下午 2:00～4:00

(有时节假日有特殊规定)

3. 票价:免费瞻仰。

三、正阳门城楼

1. 联系电话:(010)63017994

2. 开放时间:8:30～16:00

3. 票价:成人每人5元,学生每人3元。

四、人民大会堂

1. 联系电话:(010) 63096156

2. 开放时间:不固定,正常情况下与其他场馆的开放时间一致,中午休息,参观前最好电话咨询。

3. 票价: 成人每人 20 元, 学生每人10元。

五、中国历史博物馆

1. 联系电话:(010)65128321

2. 开放时间:8:30~16:30(15:30停止售票)

3. 票价:因展览内容经常更换,最好在参观前电话咨询。

六、中国革命博物馆

1. 联系电话:(010)65128967

2. 开放时间:8:30~16:30

3. 票价:因展览内容经常更换,最好在参观前电话咨询。

七、中山公园

1. 联系电话:(010) 66055431

2. 开放时间:6:00~21:00

3. 票价: 成人每人 3 元, 学生每人1.5元。

八、劳动人民文化宫

1. 联系电话:(010)65253113

2. 开放时间:6:00~21:00

3. 票价:入门票成人每人 2 元,学生每人 1元;参观中华和钟票每人 15 元;祭祖展门票每人 5 元。

九、景山公园

1. 联系电话:(010)64044071

2. 开放时间:6:00~21:00

3. 票价:成人每人 10 元,学生每人 5 元。

十、北海公园

1. 联系电话:(010)64040610

2. 开放时间:6:00~21:00

3. 票价:成人每人10元,学生每人5元,琼岛景区每人10元(含门票5元)。

明朝皇帝纪年表

（1368～1644）

姓名	年号	庙号	继位年龄	在位时间
朱元璋	洪武	太祖	41	1368～1398
朱允炆	建文		22	1398～1402
朱棣	永乐	成祖	43	1402～1424
朱高炽	洪熙	仁宗	47	1424～1425
朱瞻基	宣德	宣宗	28	1425～1435
朱祁镇	正统	英宗	9	1435～1449
朱祁钰	景泰	代宗	22	1449～1457
朱祁镇	天顺	英宗	31	1457～1464
朱见深	成化	宪宗	18	1464～1487
朱祐樘	弘治	孝宗	18	1487～1505
朱厚照	正德	武宗	15	1505～1521
朱厚熜	嘉靖	世宗	15	1521～1566
朱载坖	隆庆	穆宗	30	1566～1572
朱翊钧	万历	神宗	10	1572～1620
朱常洛	泰昌	光宗	39	1620年8～9月
朱由校	天启	熹宗	16	1620～1627
朱由检	崇祯	思宗	18	1627～1644

清朝皇帝纪年表

(1644～1912)

姓名	年号	庙号	继位年龄	在位时间
福临	顺治	世祖	6	1644～1661
玄烨	康熙	圣祖	8	1662～1722
胤禛	雍正	世宗	45	1722～1735
弘历	乾隆	高宗	25	1735～1795
颙琰	嘉庆	仁宗	37	1795～1820
旻宁	道光	宣宗	39	1820～1850
奕詝	咸丰	文宗	20	1850～1861
载淳	同治	穆宗	6	1861～1874
载湉	光绪	德宗	4	1874～1908
溥仪	宣统		3	1908～1912